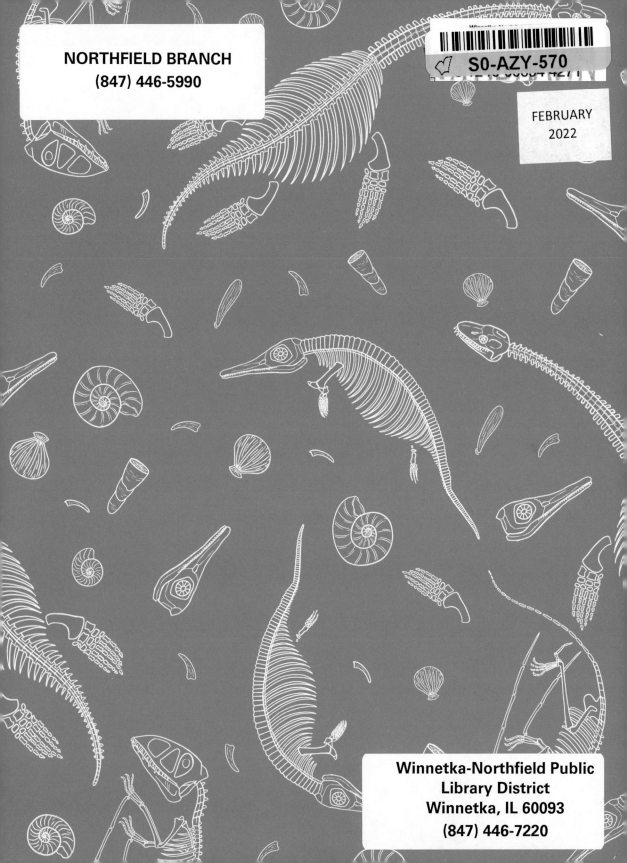

FOSSIL HUNTER

HOW MARY ANNING CHANGED THE SCIENCE OF PREHISTORIC LIFE

BY CHERYL BLACKFORD

Houghton Mifflin Harcourt
Boston   New York

hmhbooks.com

The text was set in Adobe Garamond Pro.
Cover illustration by Stephanie Son
Cover design by Celeste Knudsen
Interior design and linear fossil illustrations by Ellen Duda

The Library of Congress Cataloging-in-Publication Data is on file.
ISBN: 978-0-358-39605-5

Manufactured in China
DCP 10 9 8 7 6 5 4 3 2 1
4500833722

For Archer, Greta, Mara, and Quinn.
And for all the girls who are told "you can't."

A
DELINEATION
OF THE
STRATA
OF
ENGLAND AND WALES,
WITH PART OF
SCOTLAND;
EXHIBITING
THE COLLIERIES AND MINES,
THE MARSHES AND FEN LANDS ORIGINALLY OVERFLOWED BY THE SEA,
AND THE
VARIETIES OF SOIL
ACCORDING TO THE VARIATIONS IN THE SUBSTRATA,
ILLUSTRATED by the MOST DESCRIPTIVE NAMES
BY W. SMITH.

Lyme Regis

CONTENTS

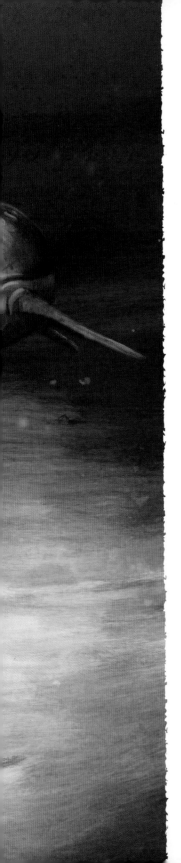

INTRODUCTION

The old ichthyosaur lay in the ooze on the rippled seabed and flapped her tail, clouding the water with muck. An ammonite drifted past. The ichthyosaur's huge eye focused one last time. Her slack jaws opened but she was too weak to catch her prey—too weak to do anything but lie in the cool deep and wait for death. She had birthed her final young, chased her final fish, and breathed her final breath.

Mud settled around the ichthyosaur's great body. Her flesh rotted, leaving only bones as evidence that she had once lived in this mysterious underwater world. More layers of mud covered her skeleton, growing thicker and thicker until sediment and bone turned to stone.

For nearly two hundred million years, the ichthyosaur's bones lay imprisoned in rock. The earth's surface changed. Rock layers crumpled and bent into mountain ranges. Volcanoes spewed lava. Earthquakes shook the ground. And the warm sea that had once been the ichthyosaur's home retreated until the rocks that hid her remains were exposed to the elements. Wind, water, and waves wore down limestone and shale, revealing precious fossil treasure in cliffs striped like a layered rock cake.

One day a girl—a curious, determined girl—saw something unusual in those cliffs near her home: an outline, a shadow . . . a great staring eye!

That girl was Mary Anning.

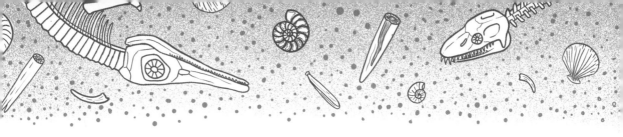

CHAPTER 1

Crocodile or Sea Monster?

A few days ago, immediately after the late high tide, was discovered, under the cliffs between Lyme Regis and Charmouth, the complete petrifaction of a crocodile, 17ft in length in a very perfect state.

Western Flying Post, November 9, 1812

Thirteen-year-old Mary Anning had been hunting for an elusive treasure for months. Day after day, in good weather and bad, she had trudged along the beach near her home, looking for any sign of fossil bones. She'd walked back and forth across the seaweed-slippery rock ledges, carefully studying the ground beneath her boots. She'd walked along the base of the Church Cliffs, hoping to find bones in the layers of limestone and shale there. But if the mystery monster fossil she was searching for was somewhere nearby, it was well hidden.

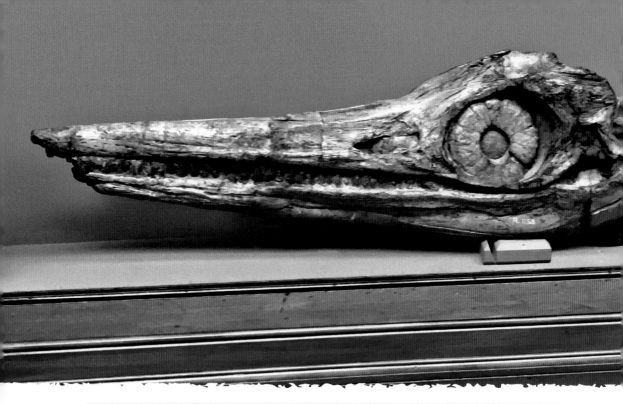

Joseph Anning found this four-foot-long fossil skull near his home in Lyme Regis; Mary Anning found the rest of the bones seen here. Some people thought the animal was a crocodile, but no crocodile has a donut-shaped ring of bones around its eyes.

The previous year Mary's older brother, Joseph, had been out fossil hunting on the beach not far from their home when he'd spied a huge fossil skull. It was so heavy that he'd needed the help of workmen to carry it home to his father's cellar workshop. Mary had studied the monster's long snout, jaw filled with big ridged teeth, and enormous eye sockets. Some people who saw the fossil wondered if it was a crocodile; Mary wondered if it had a body. She had a keen eye and a knack for discovering fossils—if the rest of the skeleton was somewhere nearby, she was determined to find it.

Joseph told Mary where he'd found the four-foot-long skull,

but she hunted for the rest of the skeleton without success. She searched for months until, one wonderful day when a winter storm had washed away part of the cliff and foreshore, she finally spied her treasure—big round vertebrae. Mary chipped away at the rock and soon found long thin ribs attached to some of the vertebrae. She spent hours on the freezing beach, patiently working to free the skeleton from the rocks that imprisoned it.

The slab of shale containing the fossil was too heavy for Mary to remove by herself, so her mother, Molly, hired workmen to cut the rock and carry the fossil back to their house. Now the Annings had the skull and the body—a skeleton that they knew was significant and must surely be worth a fortune. And they certainly needed the money. Since the death of Mary's father two years before, there had not been enough to eat in the Anning home.

Before the Annings could sell their fossil treasure, Mary had work to do. Many of the bones were hidden within the rock—if she could uncover them, the fossil would be more valuable. She had watched her father remove surplus rock with sharp chisels,

Plate 35. Vol. 3.

BULLOCK'S MUSEUM,
22, Piccadilly.

William Bullock displayed his enormous collection of natural, archaeological, and cultural objects in a museum built in 1812. People paid to view the objects on display, including stuffed animals from distant countries.

needles, and brushes, but she'd never seen him work on such a big fossil. Hour after backbreaking hour, she carefully chipped away at the skeleton, filling the cellar with gray dust as she worked to uncover the beautiful fossil bones. When she'd finished, she had a skull, ribs, shoulder blades, and sixty vertebrae. When the vertebrae were aligned as they would have been in life, the skeleton measured seventeen feet long. (Today most of the vertebrae are missing.)

The Annings' huge fossil was a puzzle to everyone who saw it. A local newspaper called it "the complete petrifaction of a crocodile." But if it was a crocodile, what was it doing in England, which had no native crocodiles? And if it wasn't a crocodile, what was it? No one knew.

What Mary's mother did know was that the unique fossil was valuable. She sold it to a local landowner, Henry Hoste Henley, for twenty-three pounds—in 1812, that was enough money to buy food for Mary's family for six months. Henry Hoste Henley later sold the skeleton to William Bullock's Museum of Natural Curiosities in London, where it was displayed to the public. In 1819, seven years after Mary had found it, William Bullock sold the fossil to the British Museum for forty-eight pounds, more than twice what Henry Hoste Henley paid the Annings.

The British Museum wanted Mary's monster fossil because it was important—it had helped spark questions among scientists about the history of life on earth. If it wasn't a crocodile but some other unknown species, why had no one ever seen living animals like it? What had happened to them? When, and how, had they become entombed in the rocks? Scientists of the time hadn't yet discovered the answers to these questions.

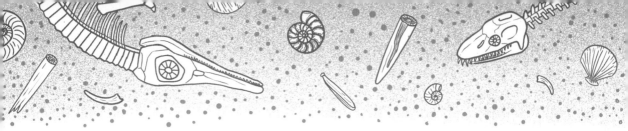

CHAPTER 2

Learning on the Beach

They was all three stricken by the Lightning on the right side of my wifes hair cap and handkerchief much burnt and the flesh wounded. The child was taken from my wifes arms and carried to its parents in appearance dead.

John Haskings, 1821

Mary Anning was born on May 21, 1799, in Lyme Regis, a small English seaside town in the county of Dorset. Although Mary's father, Richard Anning, was a skilled carpenter, the family was poor. The Annings couldn't afford to live in one of the fancy houses at the top of Lyme Regis's hills, and so they rented a wood-framed house next to the town jail in the crowded, dirty, smelly lower part of town near the river Lym. The Annings' home was squashed together with several others at the top of a vertical stone wall called the Gun Cliff—named for the military fortification placed there. The wall was all that separated the homes from the sea. On stormy days, when the sky was a threatening gray, great foaming waves pounded the Gun Cliff, sending spray over the backs of the houses.

Poor children often didn't live long in nineteenth-century England—they died from inadequate food, illness, and accidents. Several of Mary's siblings died; only Mary and her older brother, Joseph, lived to be adults. But Mary almost didn't survive her childhood. When she was nearly fifteen months old, a family friend, Elizabeth Haskings, took her to watch a horse show in a nearby field. On the stifling August day, thunder rumbled ominously over

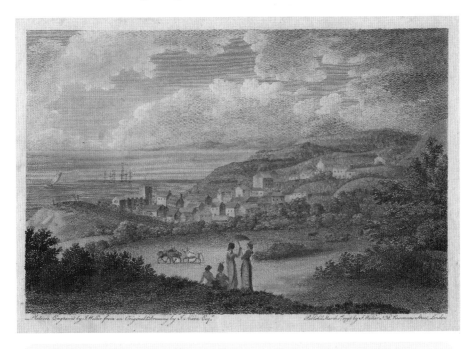

In this view of Lyme Regis, square-towered St. Michael's church is in the center left. Beyond the church are tall masts of ships anchored in the harbor. Mary Anning's first home was near the church.

Mary Anning's first home. Her parents could afford the rent because the house was located in a poor part of town.

the gathered crowd. When a sudden cloudburst drenched everyone, Elizabeth Haskings and two teenage girls ran to shelter beneath a big elm tree. After an ear-splitting thunderclap, a flash of lightning struck the tree. Elizabeth and the two girls were killed instantly, but Mary, still clasped in Elizabeth's arms, was alive. Mary's mother gently bathed her daughter in warm water to revive her. Later, local people said the lightning strike turned Mary from a sickly child into a healthy, intelligent one.

Mary's father earned money from his carpentry work and from fossils he sold on a small table in the street outside his home. The Annings were Dissenters—they did not belong to the establishment Anglican Church and instead worshipped at the Independent Chapel. After Sunday services, Richard Anning sometimes took Mary and Joseph fossil hunting, although his wife disapproved of these expeditions. They searched for fossils on the foreshore and at the Church Cliffs close to town, even though the cliffs were danger-ously unstable. The alternating layers of hard, light-gray limestone and soft, bluish-gray shale meant that huge chunks of rock often broke away from the cliffs and fell without warning to the beach below.

While Mary and Joseph hunted for fossils among sea-polished pebbles, their father split bigger rocks with quick whacks of his hammer. If he was lucky, he found a pretty amber-colored ammo-nite nestled inside. If he was unlucky, he found nothing. That's how the treasure hunting went sometimes—breaking open stone after stone and finding nothing inside.

When the tide was out, Richard, Joseph, and Mary clambered over the slippery rock ledges jutting into the bay. Removing fossils from these ledges meant a race against the sea. Once the tide turned and the sea rushed back toward the cliffs, the fossils would be cov-ered by water. Sometimes Richard walked his children half a mile east to hunt for fossils below a cliff called Black Ven. Much higher than the Church Cliffs, Black Ven towered over the beach in rows of terraces, like a giant's staircase.

In Mary's day, schools charged a fee for pupils to attend. Mary's parents could not afford to pay the fee, so the beach became her school and her father, her teacher. From him she learned to recog-nize the glint of an ammonite, the dark shine of the scales of a fossil fish, and the curve of a petrified tooth. She learned the moods and

Black Ven is 400 feet high and prone to dangerous landslides that bring mud, dirt, bushes, and trees crashing down to the beach. The golden rocks at the top are a thick layer of sandstone; beneath them are gray mudstones, marls, and shales.

tricky ways of the sea, and how to read the wind and the tides. She learned that the best time to hunt for fossils was after a storm, when the rough sea had scoured sand, gravel, and seaweed away from the rock ledges and torn loose rock from the cliffs.

One terrible day when she was ten years old, everything changed for Mary. Her father walked to nearby Charmouth, hoping to sell fossils to cross-country travelers resting there. He followed a familiar footpath through the fields above the cliffs, but then he took a shortcut that brought him dangerously close to the top of Black

Ven. No one knows why he took the shortcut—perhaps he became confused in the dim light of a sea mist—but the detour was disastrous. Mary's father slipped and tumbled partway down the cliff, hitting his head and injuring his back. Somehow he dragged himself back up to the top and stumbled home.

The frightening accident changed Mary's father mentally and physically. The big, passionate, charming man that Mary adored became weak and withdrawn and lost all interest in fossil hunting. Some days he stayed in bed, engulfed in racking fits of coughing that left smears of blood in his handkerchief. The blood was a sign of consumption (a disease we now call tuberculosis). Consumption was a killer, especially among poor people. It was a death sentence for Richard Anning.

Mary's beloved father died in late 1810, when she was eleven and he was only forty-four years old. Molly, pregnant with another child, was devastated. Mary and Joseph were bereft. The heart of their family was gone. The house was gloomy and empty without him.

Richard Anning's death was a financial disaster for his family. He owed one hundred and twenty pounds—a massive debt for a carpenter. A laborer working for two weeks might earn a single pound. How could Molly repay one hundred and twenty? But if she did not, her debtors could have her thrown in jail and her children taken from her. Molly was desperate, and so she asked the overseers

An ammonite cut in half to reveal the inner chambers. Ammonites lived on earth for 140 million years, eventually becoming extinct at about the same time as the dinosaurs. They are related to present-day squid, octopuses, and cuttlefish.

of the poor in her parish for help. They granted her a meager allowance of a few shillings a week, but it was barely enough to feed and house her children let alone pay back Richard's debt.

Not long after Richard died, Molly gave birth to a boy she named after his father. Sadly, baby Richard soon died too. Grief felled Molly; she was so devastated by the deaths of her husband and baby that she neglected her two remaining children. Mary and Joseph did what they could to help. Joseph earned pennies doing odd jobs and running errands for people until he was apprenticed to an upholsterer, where he learned how to cover sofas, chairs, and stools with fabric.

Mary ran errands too, and tried to adjust to life without the father she had idolized. She missed the time they had spent on the beach together, so one day she gathered her tools and followed the familiar footpath down to the sea. She couldn't have her father back, but she could still hunt for fossils.

Gulls wheeled overhead, battling the wind and screeching their harsh cries. Mary gripped her hammer. The beach was her territory now. She knew the best places to find fossils. She knew how to hold a stone against the ground and hit it with her hammer—*thwack*—just as her father had. She could be a fossil hunter just like him.

Mary's first really good find was a beautiful ammonite. Ammonites were common in the rocks near Lyme Regis. Some people called them snakestones because of their coiled shape. But snakes have heads; these fossils did not. And some were as big as the wheels of a cart. Mary's father had sometimes sawed ammonites in half—he knew that they had a series of internal chambers, not the vertebrae of a serpent that had been turned to stone. Mary knew that people bought these pretty fossil curiosities to display in their homes. If she put her new find on her father's little table in the street outside the workshop, someone might buy it.

Mary never did display her ammonite, because on the way home she met a well-dressed lady who bought the fossil for half a crown, which would buy a week's worth of food for the Annings, perhaps even some luxuries like tea and sugar. At eleven years old Mary had become a businesswoman. She had found a way to earn money doing something she loved—fossil hunting.

Ammonite shells were divided into internal chambers; the animal lived in the last, biggest, chamber. Ammonites used the buoyancy of the chambers to rise and sink. When they needed a burst of speed, they squirted water from an internal tube to push themselves backwards.

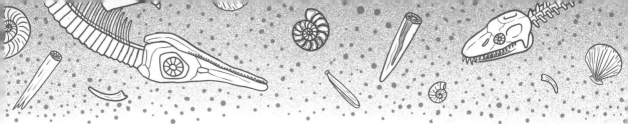

CHAPTER 3

Not a Lady

It is certainly uncommon to hear of a lady engaging in such a fatiguing, hazardous pursuit; and I think few would be found who would be willing to undertake a personal examination of the cliffs, especially in the depth of winter.

Maria Hack, 1832

As she grew older Mary Anning expanded her fossil business with the help of her mother and brother. A skilled fossil hunter like Mary could find ammonites, fish, seashells, sea lilies, and even the bones and teeth of much bigger animals in the rock layers exposed in the cliffs and on the foreshore near Lyme Regis. But out on the beach, Mary was often in danger; she had to be wary of rockfalls from cliffs weakened by rain. Black Ven, the cliff that had killed her father, was especially dangerous. In wet weather, water soaked through the ground, loosening soil and soft layers of rock and sending muddy avalanches sliding to the beach below. The sea was another danger—there were places on the beach where a careless person could easily be trapped by an incoming tide. Once trapped, the person could avoid drowning only by making a dangerous climb up the unstable cliffs. Mary could not afford to be afraid of these hazards—she had a living to make and her fossils were her only source of income.

Mary sold some of her fossils to visitors as souvenirs of their stay in Lyme Regis and others to collectors for their curiosity cabinets. Curiosity cabinets were often much more than pieces of furniture—they were whole rooms where wealthy people displayed collections of interesting objects to friends and relatives.

Mary also sold fossils to geologists who studied them to try to understand the history of living things. Most English people of the time believed what the Bible and the Anglican Church taught—that God had created the earth and all its living things. They also believed that the earth was perfect and had not changed since God made it. But Mary's fossils were of animals that didn't seem to exist anymore. If some animal species no longer existed, what had happened to them?

In the early 1800s a French scientist, Jean-Baptiste Lamarck, suggested an explanation for the missing species—he thought some animals had disappeared from the earth because they had transformed into higher forms of life through generation after generation. Life on earth had progressed over time from simple forms to complex forms in an unbroken "chain of being" ending in humans. If Lamarck was right, ammonites could no longer be found alive because they had changed over many generations into different animals better adapted to the environment. Other scientists suggested an alternative explanation. They thought that missing species had not transformed to adapt to changing conditions but had died out (become extinct) and been replaced by other animals more suited to the new conditions. These new theories sparked a great debate among religious scholars and scientists.

Mary was eager to learn as much as possible about geology and the fossils she found, but she couldn't afford to buy books or

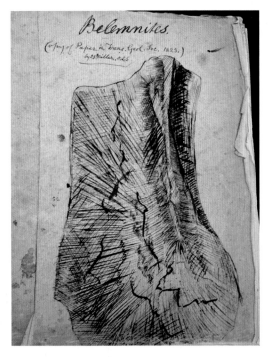 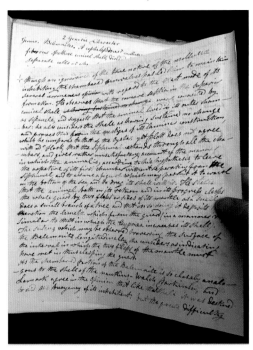

Mary Anning made this careful copy of a scientific article about fossil belemnites. Paper was expensive so she used whatever she had available – even different sizes and types.

subscriptions to scientific journals. She could not borrow books from a library either, since public libraries were not commonly available in England until the mid-1800s. And even if she could have afforded the fees, women were not allowed to attend university. So Mary educated herself by borrowing books and journals from wealthy friends and copying out articles that interested her,

including the detailed illustrations. In a letter to her friend Charlotte Murchison, the wife of the famous geologist Sir Roderick Murchison, Mary gleefully described borrowing the memoirs of three distinguished men, saying, "I do so enjoy an opposition among the big wigs."

Two of Mary's wealthy friends were Henry De La Beche and Reverend William Buckland. Both were brilliant geologists who made many remarkable contributions to the understanding of the earth's history. Mary met Henry when he arrived in Lyme Regis after

Henry De La Beche (pronounced "beach") was a brilliant geologist and a world traveler, studying geology in Britain, France, Switzerland, and Jamaica. In 1835, he was appointed the first director of the Geological Survey of Great Britain, and later he was president of the Geological Society of London.

his mother married for the third time. Mary was thirteen and poor; Henry was sixteen and independently wealthy, but he enjoyed spending time with Mary and her brother, Joseph, and soon developed a keen interest in geology. Henry and Mary became lifelong friends, and their friendship benefited both of them. Mary had practical experience and a knack for finding exceptional fossils, while Henry had the latest scientific knowledge at his fingertips, as well as wealthy acquaintances who might buy Mary's fossils.

When she was about sixteen, Mary met William Buckland when he visited Lyme Regis. William Buckland was a big, jolly man with a booming voice and quirky habits (like keeping a live hyena, called Billy, in his college rooms and using fossil vertebrae as candlesticks). He was a clergyman in the Church of England and became the first reader in geology at the famous Oxford University. Mary and William were not just friends—they discussed ideas and theories and conducted research together.

Mary was an astute businesswoman. She wrote to her wealthy buyers and piqued their interest by describing her

William Buckland with his famous blue fossil-collecting bag (and an umbrella in case of rain).

latest fossil finds with glowing phrases such as "worthy of a place in a museum," "perfect as if just taken from a dissecting room," and "as perfect as any fossil I ever saw." Despite having no formal training, she described the anatomy of her fossils in scientific terms and included excellent sketches of her finds.

But Mary had learned to read and write at Sunday school and was self-conscious about her misspellings and poor grammar. In a postscript to a letter to her friend Charlotte Murchison, Mary wrote,

I believe the best thing is to advise your throwing this into the fire without reading and as a appolige [apology] for not writing a better I beg to say I have walked ten miles today I am so tired I can scarcely old [hold] the pen.

The British social class system meant that rich people did not befriend poor people. Mary was an exception to this rule, and her wealthy friends included a few ladies. Mary herself would never be mistaken for a "lady." She was thin and muscular, with dirt crusting her hands and fingernails. Her cheeks were reddened by wind and rain. She didn't dress in the flimsy fabrics and tight fashions of the day but instead wore comfortable layers of warm, sturdy clothing. Instead of dainty shoes she wore tough leather footwear and occasionally *pattens* (little platforms that buckled onto her shoes and lifted her feet above the mud). And instead of wearing fashionable curls framing her face, Mary pulled her hair into a practical bun and tucked it beneath a

Journal des Modes – Paris 1820

Anna Maria Pinney pasted these drawings of Paris fashions from 1820 into her scrapbook. The women are wearing expensive, stylish outdoor and indoor clothing that Mary Anning could not have afforded to buy.

bonnet. To protect her head from falling rocks, she sometimes wore a battered felt top hat coated with layers of varnish to harden it.

One of Mary's lady friends was Elizabeth Philpot, a resident of Lyme Regis. Elizabeth and her two sisters had a large collection of fossils that they kept in cabinets in their cluttered home. Selina Hallet, another Lyme Regis resident, noted about the Philpots,

They were great fossilists and had a very large collection. Several cases with glass tops and shallow drawers all down the front stood in the dining room, and the back parlour, and upstairs on the landing, all full of fossils with a little ticket on each of them.

Like Mary, Elizabeth didn't mind getting muddy in the hunt for exciting fossils. And like Mary, she was interested in learning more about her finds. It's not surprising that the two women became friends.

In this portrait of Mary Anning, painted after her death, she holds her rock hammer and fossil-collecting basket and points to an ammonite while her dog, Tray, lies nearby. It was common for subjects not to smile in portraits of the time.

Another of Mary's wealthy friends was Anna Maria Pinney. Anna Maria met Mary when her family visited Lyme Regis in 1831. The Pinney family owned sugar plantations in the West Indies, where they enslaved their workers. Anna Maria, twelve years younger than Mary, was educated and refined, but she had an adventurous streak and was interested in science and nature, so Mary took her fossil hunting. One windy day Mary and Anna Maria set out for the beach before the tide had turned. When they reached the bottom of the steep, slippery path, they found that the tide hadn't yet receded and there was only a narrow strip of dry land between the foot of the cliffs and the sea. If they had walked any farther, a sudden big wave could have smashed them into the rocks or dragged them down into the surf. Mary was so strong that she simply seized Anna Maria around her waist and carried her to a safer part of the beach "with the same ease as you would a baby."

Anna Maria described Mary as kind, affectionate, and generous to people in need. But she also noted that Mary was proud and preferred spending time with her educated friends rather than with people from her own social class. Anna Maria wrote of Mary in her journal:

> *She has been noticed by all the cleverest men in England. . . . This has completely turned her head, and she has the proudest and most unyielding spirit I have ever met with . . . she glories in being afraid of no one, and in saying everything she pleases. . . . Associating and being courted by those above her, she frankly owns that the society of her own rank is become distasteful to her.*

However much Mary's friends admired her skill, they did not see her as their equal. Trapped between two worlds, she did not seem to fit in either.

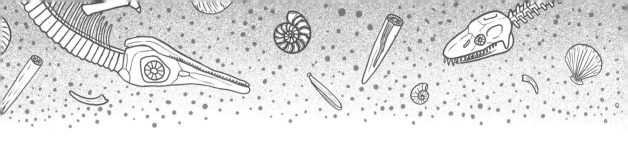

CHAPTER 4

Geological Mysteries

The extraordinary thing in this young woman is that she has made herself so thoroughly acquainted with the science that the moment she finds any bones she knows to what tribe they belong.

Lady Harriet Silvester, 1824

The monster fossil that Mary and Joseph Anning found when they were children puzzled scientists for years—it was unlike any known living animal. It had a long, pointed snout like a crocodile, but no crocodile had huge saucer eyes with a ring of bony plates around them. And no crocodile had its nostrils set near its eyes instead of at the end of its snout. The animal had a long, slender backbone like a fish but a chest like a lizard. And its four limbs were packed with rows of small bones and looked more like flippers than legs.

But if Mary's monster was not a crocodile, what was it? Not even the experts knew.

In 1817, Charles Konig (the curator at the British Museum) finally gave monsters like Mary's a name—*Ichthyosaurus* (from the Latin words for *fish* and *lizard*). After years of arguments, scientists decided that the anatomy of Mary's fossil showed that it was an air-breathing reptile. But what had happened to these reptiles? If, as Jean Baptiste-Lamarck thought, animals changed from one species to another in a continuous progression, where did Mary's ichthyosaur fit? When had it lived on the earth? What went before it and what came after it? And if Lamarck was wrong, what other explanation could there be for these missing reptiles?

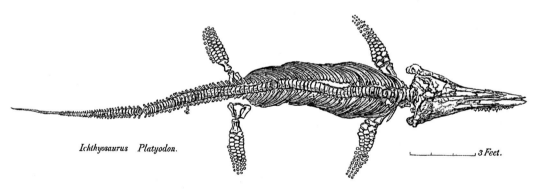

Ichthyosaurus Platyodon.

3 Feet.

This drawing of an Ichthyosaurus platyodon *fossil shows its sinuous shape, long tail, and elongated jaw filled with sharp teeth. Unlike crocodiles (which have limbs with pronounced digits) this animal has four paddle-like limbs formed from rows of small bones.*

When she was nineteen, Mary found another rare complete ichthyosaur and sold it to Lieutenant Colonel Thomas Birch, a fossil collector. But after that she didn't find any exceptional fossils for many months, and her family was soon penniless again. The finances of the Anning family were like a roller coaster, with peaks when Mary had something extraordinary to sell and sharp dips when she found no new fossils or no one wanted to buy the fossils she had. In desperation, Mary's mother decided to sell their furniture to pay the rent. When Colonel Birch found out about the Anning family's plight he was shocked. Mary had made such important fossil discoveries—how could she be penniless? In March 1820, he wrote to the geologist Gideon Mantell:

> *I am going to sell my collection for the benefit of the poor woman Molly and her son Joseph and daughter Mary at Lyme who have in truth found almost all the fine things, which have been submitted to scientific investigation. . . . I may never again possess what I am about to part with; yet in doing it I shall have the satisfaction of knowing that the money will be well applied.*

Birch had spent years, and much money, gathering his collection. His fossils were auctioned at Bullock's Museum in London. Collectors traveled miles to the sale—some coming by ship from as far away as the European continent. The auction raised over four hundred pounds—a fortune for the Annings.

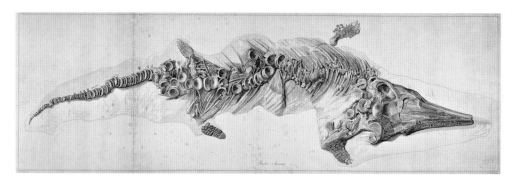

This exquisite drawing of a fossil owned by Thomas Birch, and later sold at auction, shows the ichthyosaur lying belly down, revealing its round, concave vertebrae, slim ribs, tooth-filled jaws, and four limbs.

In May 1821, a year after the auction, Mary found a beautiful five-foot-long *Ichthyosaurus communis*. Her friend Henry De La Beche reported the find to the keeper at the British Museum, hoping that the museum would buy it from her. But the museum chose to buy a cheaper fossil from her instead. Even then, they did not pay their bill on time. Molly Anning, mindful that the money from Colonel Birch's auction would not last forever, wrote them a stern letter.

> *As I am a widow woman and my chief dependence for supporting my family being the sale of fossils, I hope you will not be offended by my writing to receive the money for the last fossil as I asure [sic] you Sir I stand much in need of it.*

Mary's *Ichthyosaurus communis* was eventually bought by nine men who donated it to the Bristol Institution for the Advancement of Science, Literature, and the Arts. But it was the fossil collector George Cumberland who publicly praised Mary for her finds by writing about her in a local newspaper:

This persevering female has for years gone daily in search of fossil remains of importance at every tide, for many miles under the hanging cliffs at Lyme . . . to her exertions we owe nearly all the fine specimens of Ichthyosauri.

The next ichthyosaur Mary found was almost twenty feet long, but before she could sell it she had the difficult task of removing the matrix—or surplus rock—from around its bones. This skilled, time-consuming work, which she called "picking," made her eyes sore and could be dangerous—a careless slip of her chisel could cause a nasty gash, and flying rock chips could injure her eyes. Even though she did it by lamplight with simple tools such as hammers, chisels, brushes, and needles, Mary's work was excellent. She soon became an expert in ichthyosaur anatomy.

Mary's twenty-foot ichthyosaur was an *Ichthyosaurus platyodon,* the same species as the first one she and Joseph had found when they were children. She soon found two more ichthyosaurs, making four in twelve months.

The fossil-bearing limestones, shales, and mudstones in the cliffs near Lyme Regis were exposed in layers, called strata, piled one on top of another. Some of the layers were thick and some were thin. Some contained ichthyosaur bones; some did not. Why were the rock layers so different, and why didn't they all contain the same fossils? Mary had found fossil seashells, fish, starfish, and sea lilies in rocks that came from cliffs high above the sea. How did they get there? How had sea levels changed that much over time? While Mary worked tirelessly to find her fossils, geologists studied them to try to solve these mysteries.

The geologists who bought Mary's fossils were eager to make a name for themselves; they wanted to be the first to identify an unknown animal. They gave lectures and published scientific papers about their findings, but they rarely gave Mary the credit she deserved for discovering the fossils that made their work possible. This lack of recognition by men who had far better circumstances in life than she did frustrated Mary. Anna Maria Pinney wrote,

Ichthyosaurs lived from 250 to 90 million years ago. They were air-breathing marine reptiles with a sleek streamlined shape built for speed. This ichthyosaur has bitten through an ammonite's shell to get to the soft juicy body inside.

[Mary] says the world has used her ill . . . these men of learning have sucked her brains, and made a great deal by publishing works, of which she furnished the contents, while she derived none of the advantages.

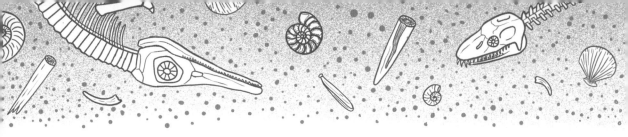

CHAPTER 5

A Second Sea Monster

It is large and heavy but one thing I may venture to assure you it is the first and only one discovered in Europe.

Mary Anning

In the early 1800s, geology was a new science and geologists had more questions than answers about the history of the earth. They knew that the earth had changed over time and was still changing. Earthquakes and volcanoes pushed up new mountains. Wind, water, and ice eroded rocks and carried away the resulting material to be deposited somewhere else as sediment, such as sand and mud. As time passed, that sediment hardened into layers of new rock. Different types of sediment formed different types of rock. When the new rock was eroded, the cycle began again.

In 1650, an Irish bishop named James Ussher had used information in the Bible to calculate that the earth was six thousand years

Alternating bands of hard, light-gray limestone and softer, dark-gray shale in the cliffs near Lyme Regis. The rock layers at the bottom of the pile were formed before, and are therefore older than, the layers at the top.

old, but over a hundred years later, in 1795, the Scottish geologist James Hutton noted that the cycle of erosion and deposition was so slow that the earth must be *millions* of years old, not just thousands. Hutton also provided evidence that rocks were not all formed at the same time—he described places where seams of granite cut through other rocks. If existing rocks had granite pushed into them, then the granite must be younger than those rocks.

Geologists proposed new theories and argued about them at rowdy meetings of the Geological Society of London. Founded in 1807 by a group of thirteen men over dinner, the Society had four hundred male members by 1818. Even if Mary Anning could have afforded to travel to London for the meetings, she would not have been allowed to join the Society—the first female member was not elected until a hundred years later. Mary had to rely on her geologist friends and their published papers for information about the latest geological theories.

The geologists Henry De La Beche, Mary's childhood friend, and William Conybeare, a clergyman, were members of the Geological Society. They had worked together to identify a strange sea creature from a handful of fossil bones. They called the animal *Plesiosaurus* (meaning *near lizard* or *almost lizard* in Latin). But because no one had unearthed a complete *Plesiosaurus* skeleton, other geologists were skeptical of their findings.

On December 10, 1823, Mary set out after a storm, hoping that the winter waves had uncovered more fossils. A bitter wind knifed through her clothes as she walked the half mile to Black Ven. Standing at the base of the menacing cliffs responsible for her father's death, she studied the black muck the rain had loosened. Something in the mudstone drew her attention—something that could be part of a fossil. Mary carefully scraped away the soft dark rock and found a skull. But the skull was short and stubby—nothing like that of an ichthyosaur. Mary raced back to town to find help before the sea could wash away her treasure. She and her helpers worked well into the night, digging in the cold December darkness. They found vertebrae, a pelvis, a jumble of ribs, and paddle-like limbs. Despite aching muscles and fingers numbed by cold, they didn't stop until they had retrieved the fossil.

Mary's new fossil was nine feet long and six feet wide, but the skull was only about seven inches long. The mystery animal had approximately ninety vertebrae, with about thirty-five of those in its very long neck. It had a stubby tail and four limbs filled with rows of short hourglass-shaped bones. Its head, body, and tail looked as though they belonged to a turtle. But what turtle had such a long neck? What turtle had limbs with rows and rows of short bones? No one had ever seen a living animal like Mary's new find. William Buckland described the unique fossil this way:

> To the head of the Lizard it united the teeth of the Crocodile; a neck of enormous length, resembling the body of a Serpent: a trunk and tail having the proportions of an ordinary quadruped, the ribs of a Camelion, and the paddles of a Whale.

Mary's fascinating new find was identified as the first complete *Plesiosaurus* anyone had ever seen. Determined to sell it for the best possible price, she included a drawing of it in the letter she wrote to prospective buyers. When he heard about the fossil, William Conybeare was so excited to have his earlier claims validated that he abandoned the sermon he was writing for his next church service and hurried to Bristol to spread the news.

One important person was not excited by Mary's latest find. Georges Cuvier, a famous French anatomist, thought Mary's

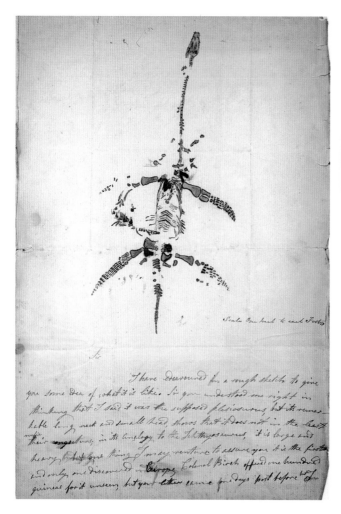

Plesiosaurus was a fake. He did not believe that an animal could have a neck with thirty-five vertebrae. After all, giraffes have only seven vertebrae in their necks and ostriches only nineteen. Georges Cuvier thought Mary must have attached the head and neck of a sea serpent to the body of an ichthyosaur to create her new fossil. This was terrible news for Mary. If people believed the fossil was a fake, her business would be ruined.

Mary sold the fossil to the Duke of Buckingham for somewhere between one hundred and two hundred pounds—an astronomical price for a fossil in those days. The duke sent it to the Geological Society in London, where William Conybeare planned to unveil the magnificent specimen to an astonished crowd of his geologist

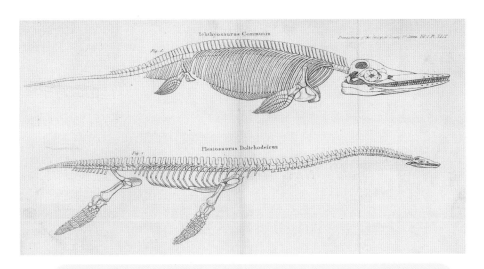

This comparison of an ichthyosaur and a plesiosaur, published in a paper by William Conybeare, clearly shows the differences in head size and neck and tail length of the two species.

colleagues. The precious fossil was enclosed in a wooden case ten feet tall by six feet wide and shipped to London by sea. Unfortunately, the ship was delayed and the plesiosaur did not arrive in time for William Conybeare's lecture—he had to be content with showing the audience a drawing.

When he described the fossil to his rapt audience William Conybeare took all the glory for himself. He did not explain that Mary Anning had both found and prepared the plesiosaur. However, Georges Cuvier later acknowledged that he had made a mistake—Mary's fossil was not a fake. Her reputation and her business were safe.

Plesiosaurs lived from 200 to 66 million years ago and were unlike any marine animal today. They were wide and round like a turtle, had improbably long necks and small heads, breathed air, and gave birth to live young. Scientists think they swam by flapping their front flippers to create a wake that gave their back flippers more power. This Attenborosaurus conybeari *was about sixteen feet long.*

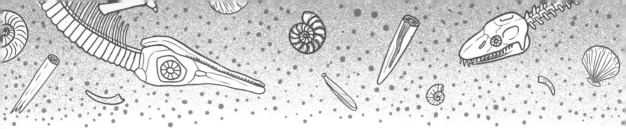

CHAPTER 6

A New Home

A plain unpretending little shop . . . richly stored with
precious specimens of the saurians, . . . it was a frequent
resort of many of the most eminent scientists of the time.

Lyme resident, 1840

Storms brought pounding waves that battered the beaches and cliffs
around Lyme Regis and exposed long-hidden fossils for hunters to
find. But storms also brought flooding to the town. One November
day in 1824, threatening clouds gathered over the southern coast
of England. When the storm broke, drenching rain drummed on
roofs and windows. The wind howled and strengthened, first to a
gale and then to the terrifying force of a hurricane. The Annings
cowered in their house as waves pounded the sea wall. Would the
wall breach and let the sea pour in? Would the wind force waves up
the river Lym and flood the lower part of town?

Angry waves beat relentlessly against the Cobb—a long curved stone wall that protected the harbor—and finally flowed right over the top, washing away a huge portion of the wall, as well as nearby houses. The Cobb had protected the harbor for hundreds of years, but it was wrecked in one night. At four o'clock in the morning, the Annings' fears were realized when the sea swirled through the lower floors of their home. As the storm raged on, ships at sea were tossed like toys in a tub. Some foundered and sank, drowning passengers and sailors in the freezing water. The *Unity* was driven ashore below Black Ven; her terrified crew had tied themselves into the rigging to prevent themselves from being washed overboard, and were rescued at low tide.

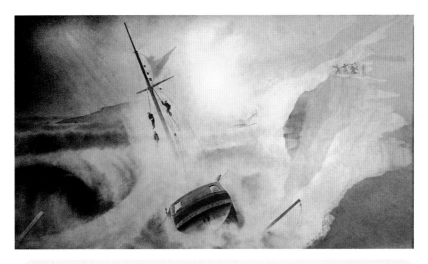

The violent storm of 1824 that wreaked havoc along the South coast of England drove the Unity *ashore below Black Ven.*

When the storm finally blew itself out the next day, the seawall protecting homes had been washed away, and the backs of many houses destroyed. Mary Anning described the chaos in a letter to a friend:

> *What a sense of horror we have gone through at Lyme. . . . Every bit of the walk from the Assembly rooms to the Cobb is gone and all the back parts of the houses on the shore side of town. . . . All the coal cellars and coals being gone and the Cobb so shattered that no vessel will be safe here, we are obliged to sit without fires this winter, a cold prospect you will allow.*

If ships could no longer moor in the harbor, coal could not be delivered to Lyme Regis. But coal was the townspeople's primary source of fuel. Families like Mary's were facing a bleak winter.

The Annings survived the cold winter, but they needed to find a new home safe from flooding. Mary was twenty-seven when her family finally moved to a house up the hill on Broad Street, not far from the cottage where her friend Elizabeth Philpot lived. Broad Street was the main shopping thoroughfare in Lyme Regis—it was an excellent location for a fossil shop. Two windows at the front of the house were perfect for displaying fossils. Mary shared the house with her mother and brother until Joseph and his new wife, Amelia, moved into their own home.

Sea lilies (crinoids) are animals not plants—they are related to starfish and sea urchins. A long stem attaches adult crinoids to floating wood or the sea bottom. The mouth at the top of the stem is surrounded by arms that gather plankton for food. In this photograph of a fossil crinoid you can clearly see the stem and feathery arms.

Mary called her shop the Fossil Depot. It was popular with visitors and with local children, who clutched their coins as they sorted through trays of ammonites, belemnites, sea lilies, and fossil seashells.

Mary was patient with her young customers and didn't seem to mind that they had little money to spend.

She would serve us with the sweetest temper, bearing with all our little fancies and never finding us too troublesome as we turned over her trays of curiosities, and concluded by spending a few pence only.

Most working women of Mary's social class labored for little pay in factories, on farms, and as servants in rich people's homes. But Mary was different—she had carved out a career doing something she loved and was now the proud proprietor of her own fossil shop.

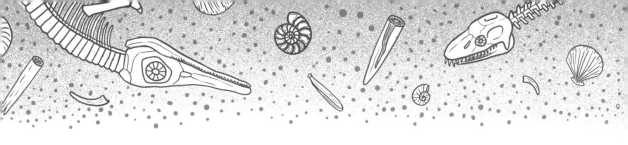

CHAPTER 7

More Important Fossils

A monster resembling nothing that has ever been seen or heard-of upon earth, excepting the dragons of romance and heraldry.

Georges Cuvier

Fossil hunting was a lonely occupation for Mary until the day a shaggy, floppy-eared black-and-white terrier called Tray joined her family. While Mary worked, Tray nosed among the seaweed or chased the gulls. And when Mary discovered an extra-big fossil, Tray stood guard until she found someone to help her carry it home.

Mary drew this sketch of her dog, Tray, on a blank page at the beginning of her copy of a scientific paper.

Not all of Mary's exciting fossils were big. Dark cylindrical stones with rounded ends, some with spiral markings on their surface, were common on the beach at Lyme Regis. Known as bezoar stones because they looked like the gallstones of bezoar goats, the stones could be found in the cliffs, too. Mary knew they were most common in the rock layers containing ichthyosaur and plesiosaur fossils. She had even found bezoar stones in the abdomens and pelvises of ichthyosaurs, which indicated to her that they were the fossilized remains of food the animals had digested. If Mary was right and bezoar stones *were* fossilized feces, they would hold important clues about the food ichthyosaurs and plesiosaurs ate, and teach scientists about the ecosystem where these animals lived.

Mary's friend William Buckland agreed with her

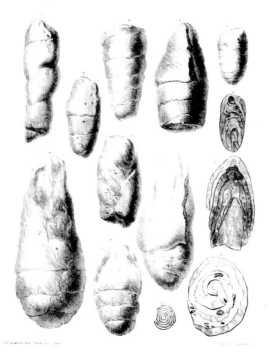

Coprolites and Sections of Coprolites from the lias at Lyme Regis. Natural size

Before photographs were invented, skilled artists made beautiful drawings of fossils to illustrate scientific papers. These coprolite drawings, used to illustrate a paper written by William Buckland, clearly show the spiral markings left by the animals' intestines.

that bezoar stones were fossilized feces—their spiral markings were the imprints of intestines.

He renamed the stones *coprolites* (from the Greek words for *manure* and *stone*). Ichthyosaur coprolites contained fish scales, the remains of belemnites, and sometimes even the bones and teeth of small ichthyosaurs—evidence that they were fearsome predators, chasing and eating whatever they could snatch in their snapping jaws.

A big ichthyosaur preys on a smaller one. Rings of bones protected ichthyosaurs' eyes from water pressure when they dove. Scientists think ichthyosaurs had a layer of blubber beneath their skin for insulation (like whales).

In one of his scientific papers William Buckland praised Mary for her fine fossils and noted that she had found coprolites "within the ribs or near the pelvis of almost every perfect skeleton of *Ichthyosaurus* she has ever found." Preserved poop had brought Mary some well-deserved recognition.

Mary had the natural curiosity of a scientist. She sometimes dissected dead animals, such as cuttlefish, to study their anatomy. Cuttlefish squirt ink to protect themselves from predators, and Mary saw oval ink sacs inside their bodies. She found similar black, shiny, sac-like objects in the rocks that contained fossil belemnites. Belemnites—squid-like creatures with a hard internal skeleton called a rostrum—were common fossils in the rocks near Lyme Regis. Had belemnites squirted ink to shield themselves from predators?

The long, slender internal skeleton, or rostrum, was the part of a belemnite most often preserved as a fossil; the animal's soft body parts were rarely preserved.

Mary and William Buckland both thought the black shiny objects were fossilized belemnite ink sacs, but they had no proof until several years later when Louis Agassiz, a famous Swiss geologist, spotted two belemnites with their ink sacs inside them in the fossil collection of the Philpot sisters, Mary's friends. Mary and William Buckland were right—belemnites did squirt ink.

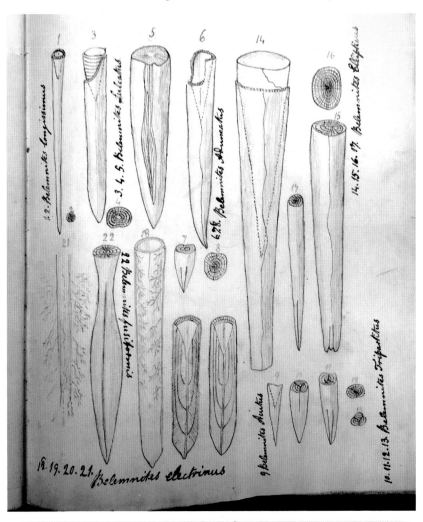

Mary Anning copied these drawings of belemnite rostra from a scientific paper.

Belemnites lived on earth for about 135 million years, finally becoming extinct about 66 million years ago. Agile and free swimming, they squirted clouds of ink to hide themselves from predators. The ten arms surrounding their heads had tiny hooks to snag prey that they then crushed in their strong beak-like jaws.

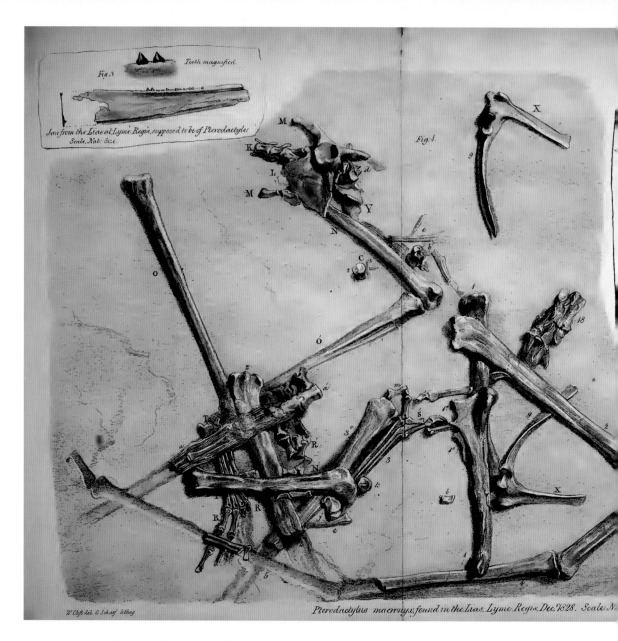

Pterodactylus macronyx, found in the Lias, Lyme Regis, Dec.r 1828. Scale N.

On a cold, clear December day in 1828, Mary was fossil hunting on the beach with Tray when she found an unusual fossil. She freed the slab containing her find and took it home. Mary's new treasure was a jumble of bones with no skull. In the raven-size skeleton Mary recognized vertebrae, ribs, legs, feet, and very

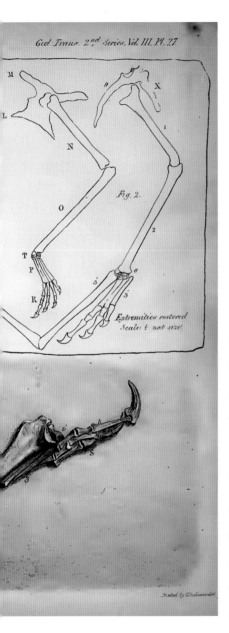

Fig. 2.

Extremities restored
Scale ⅓ nat size

Printed by C. Hullmandel

Mary Anning's Pterodactylus macronyx *(later renamed* Dimorphodon macronyx*). Apart from the missing skull, it is an almost complete skeleton. Complete pterodactyl fossils are rare; the animals usually died on land where their carcasses were eaten by scavengers and their fragile bones broken and scattered.*

odd fingers. Three of the fingers on each arm were short and hooked at the end like claws, but the fourth finger was longer than the rest of the arm.

Similar fossil reptiles had been found in Germany. These strange creatures had bodies and tails like those of mammals, but their skulls were small and reptilian with huge eyes. And in what looked like a bird's beak were rows of lethal sharp teeth. Georges Cuvier, the French anatomist, named these nightmarish flying reptiles *Pterodactyles* (from the Greek words for *wing* and *finger*). Mary was the first person to find a pterodactyl in England. William Buckland named her fossil *Pterodactylus macronyx* and credited her with this momentous find in a paper he presented to the Geological Society in 1829.

Pterodactylus macronyx *(now* Dimorphodon macronyx*) lived about 200 million years ago. It had a big head, two types of teeth (for catching and eating its prey) and a long tail that probably stabilized it in flight. Scientists think Dimorphodon could climb trees and feasted on insects and small land vertebrates. Pterodactyls are a genus of pterosaur—the first flying vertebrates on earth.*

A year after finding the pterodactyl, on another chilly December day, something in the sticky mud at the foot of Black Ven attracted Mary's attention. She dug until her hands and hem were caked with mud. She only stopped digging when the sea threatened to cut her off from home. Mary gathered what she could of her fossil, whistled to Tray and hurried back to Lyme Regis. The next day people gathered to watch her look for the rest of her treasure, but if they were expecting something big they were disappointed. The new fossil was only about eighteen inches long.

Mary sent prospective buyers a drawing showing her new fossil's big eye sockets, delicate backbone, and long snout with a spike above it, but noted that she had not yet found the tail. She knew her fossil was unique and described it in a letter to Adam Sedgwick, a professor of geology at Cambridge University:

A head like a pair of scissors Vertebrae like an encrenite [a crinoid or sea lily] thin as a thread of which there are two 100 & 52 and the tail wanting the greater portion of six claws or felers [feelers] and winged like fins . . . being the only one in Europe 50 £.

A rich landowner eventually bought Mary's fossil even though it was missing its tail. (The Philpot sisters later acquired the tail but refused to sell it to him.) Scientists decided that Mary's new fossil was a fish with a skeleton made of cartilage and gave it the grand name *Squaloraja polyspondyla* (meaning a shark/ray with many vertebrae). Mary was the first person in the world to find a squaloraja fossil.

Mary was only twenty-nine years old and had made four momentous fossil finds:

- the world's most complete ichthyosaur with con-nected bones;
- the world's first complete plesiosaur;
- the first pterodactyl found in Britain; and
- the world's first squaloraja.

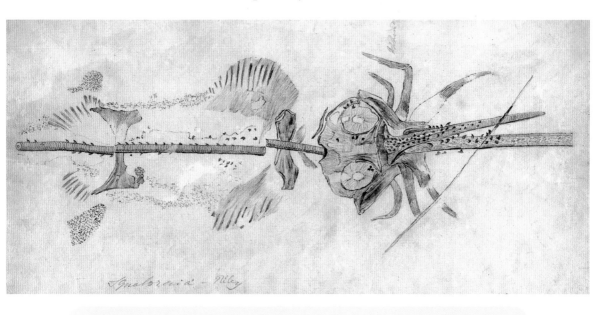

Mary Anning's Squaloraja polyspondyla *fossil had a big head, two large eye sockets, a long jaw with a frontal spine sticking out above it, and a long thin backbone with about 260 vertebrae. Along each side of the spine were the faint impressions of wing-like fins.*

Squaloraja *lived about 200 million years ago. They had skeletons made of cartilage, not bone. Their fins probably helped them swim close to the sea floor with a graceful "flying" motion like modern stingrays. Only the males had long frontal spines.*

Mary knew the rocks of Lyme Regis better than anyone and was skilled at finding and preparing fossils. Her discoveries were of huge importance to geologists working to understand the geology of England and the history of life on earth—they proved that a sea teeming with strange animals had once covered the lush countryside and rolling hills around Lyme Regis. Fish with thick armor-like scales swam in that sea; ammonites and belemnites bobbed in its water—their soft muscular bodies providing tempting morsels for predatory ichthyosaurs and plesiosaurs.

Pterodactyls dominated the air near the seashore and geologists were finding evidence of other mysterious land monsters. In 1824, at the same meeting where William Conybeare described Mary's first *Plesiosaurus,* William Buckland displayed fossil bones from a huge terrestrial reptile he named *Megalosaurus.* Other geologists later found similar massive fossil bones and teeth, but it wasn't until 1842 that the English scientist Richard Owen named these huge land reptiles *Dinosauria,* or *terrible lizards.* At the time Owen named the dinosaurs, scientists were still arguing about what had caused the disappearance of animal species such as ichthyosaurs, plesiosaurs, ammonites, and belemnites.

Mary's fossil finds were proof that a sea filled with strange animals had once covered the countryside around her home. In this illustration of a similar sea, a plesiosaur chases a belemnite while other belemnites, ammonites, and fish swim nearby. Ammonite shells and pieces of wood litter the sea floor; over time they will become fossils.

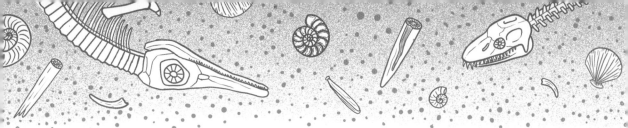

CHAPTER 8

From Excitement to Heartache

It is without exception the most beautiful fossil I have ever seen.

Mary Anning

Mary's daily life was one of hard work and danger. She had little opportunity to escape her responsibilities until the day in 1829 when her friend Charlotte Murchison invited her to London. Mary was thirty and, like most poor people in England, had never traveled very far from her home. She was eager to see London's grand buildings, beautiful churches, private collections, and magnificent British Museum.

One exciting day Mary left her home and traveled east, either by boat or by horse-drawn coach. As she neared London she saw elegant mansions with beautiful gardens, but then the peaceful scene changed to one of industrial warehouses, factories, and humble dwellings crowded together. Hawkers selling their wares rang bells and shouted as people hurried through the busy streets. Horses whinnied and carriages rattled past, churning up dust. The air was rank with the stink of raw sewage and black with the soot of factories and thousands of coal fires.

In the record she kept of her visit Mary described the British Museum, where she saw ancient Egyptian sculptures, beautiful old royal prayer books, and the King's Library with more than sixty thousand books. She toured the Geological Society rooms at Somerset House where her host, Mr. Lonsdale, showed her fossils, stuffed animals, and a model of one of her plesiosaur fossils that had been sent to Paris, France. She thought the plesiosaur model was so well done that she "could barely distinguish its difference" from the real thing. Mary saw the skeleton of a bat that reminded her of her pterodactyl.

London, 1827. When Mary visited London it was the biggest city in the world with almost two million residents. Tall narrow buildings crowded together, many with cellars, small shops at the street level, apartments above the shops, and servants' quarters in the attics.

She also saw some of her own fossil finds. If Mary was disappointed that her name did not appear on any of the fossil labels—only the names of the men who had donated them—she did not say in the notes she wrote about her visit.

The trip to London was a break from the predictable rhythms of Mary's home life—fossil hunting when the weather and sea allowed and working in the shop when they did not. But as soon as she returned home, Mary resumed her daily routines. December is a good month for fossil hunting near Lyme Regis; winter storms batter the cliffs, breaking off chunks of rock and exposing fossils that have been hidden for millions of years. In December 1830, Mary discovered a lovely plesiosaur. It lay curled in its bed of rock as though resting—its long neck curved in a graceful arc. Mary counted over fifty vertebrae in the neck and spine. She found three of the animal's four paddle-like limbs, but the most amazing thing about Mary's new fossil was the size of its skull—much bigger in relation to its body than those of the other plesiosaurs she had found.

Eager to find a buyer for her fossil, Mary wrote to her old friend William Buckland. If he did not want to buy the plesiosaur, she knew he could find someone who would.

It is without exception the most beautiful fossil I have ever seen. The tail and one paddle is wanting (which I hope to get at the first rough sea) every bone is in place, in short if it had been made of wax it could not be more beautiful, but I should remark that the head is twice as large in proportion as those I have hitherto found.

Mary sold her beautiful plesiosaur to Lord Cole (the Earl of Enniskillen) for two hundred and twenty pounds, a fabulous sum for one fossil. Richard Owen named the new species *Plesiosaurus macrocephalus* (meaning *large head* or *long head* in Greek). In a paper he published about the fossil, Owen thanked Lord Cole and praised a fossil collector named Thomas Hawkins for his knowledge of plesiosaurs. But he did not mention Mary.

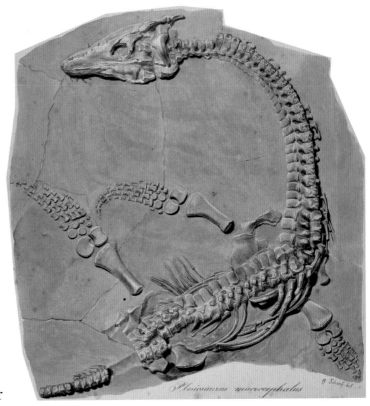

Painting of Mary Anning's "most beautiful" fossil. The Plesiosaurus macrocephalus *was a juvenile, only about four and a half feet long, but with an exceptionally large head for a plesiosaur.*

Thomas Hawkins played an important role in another

disappointment for Mary. In July 1832, she was hunting for fossils in a jutting section of cliff near her home when she found a five-foot-long ichthyosaur skull—the biggest anyone had ever seen. If the skull was that big, Mary knew the rest of the animal must be huge. She dug deeper into the rocks, but the fossil was buried beyond her reach and she could not afford to hire workmen to help her retrieve it—the fossil would have to stay buried.

Hawkins arrived in Lyme Regis on the day that Mary found the enormous skull. He immediately bought it from her, but he was not content to have only the skull—he wanted the rest of the fossil too. Mary warned him that the skeleton was buried beneath tons of rock, but he ignored her and hired a gang of workmen. For two days the men hacked at the cliff with pickaxes, sledgehammers, and rock chisels, and removed load after load of rubble. On the third day the workmen finally found the fossil. But when they tried to remove it, the soft rock crumbled. They had dug out twenty thousand loads of rock and removed a whole section of cliff, but all Hawkins had left were six hundred ichthyosaur bone fragments. He later wrote,

With the kind assistance of Miss Anning, the whole of them [the bones] were packed, and by night-fall the last heavy box-full was deposited in a place of safety. So secured the skeleton and its matrix weighed a ton.

The fossil's bones and rock matrix weighed about as much as an adult hippopotamus—preparing and reassembling the fragments was a monumental task. Hawkins glued the pieces together and cemented the finished fossil into a huge wooden case. It was the biggest *Ichthyosaurus platyodon* anyone had ever found.

Hawkins liked his fossils to look as complete as possible and sometimes sneakily filled in missing bones with replicas made of plaster. Mary was a scientist at heart; she disapproved of altering fossils this way, even though that might have brought her better prices. She wrote about Hawkins:

> *He makes things as he imagines they ought to be; and not as they are really found, the platyodon that I in part gave him was [too] large for my poverty & I would not have trusted to his making up, though very much broken it might be made a splendid thing without any addition.*

As she feared he would, Hawkins recreated the missing fourth paddle of his ichthyosaur. His wealth had bought him a prize that Mary could not afford, but he could not resist "improving" it.

In October 1833, over a year after discovering the huge ichthyosaur, Mary was fossil hunting with Tray when something terrible happened. Chunks of rock crashed down the cliff without warning, smashed into a pile on the beach, and killed her little dog. Mary was devastated. She later wrote to her friend Charlotte Murchison to tell her the dreadful news:

My Dear Madam, I would have answered your kind letter by the return of post, if I had been able. Perhaps you will laugh when I say that the death of my old faithful dog quite upset me, the Cliff fell upon him and killed him in a moment before my eyes, and close to my feet, it was but a moment between me and the same fate.

Mary was fortunate not to be crushed by the rocks that killed Tray. Two months later she was lucky again when she survived a dangerous collision with a runaway cart. If she'd been seriously injured in either of these accidents, it would have ended her fossil-hunting career.

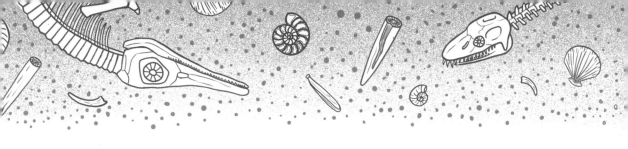

CHAPTER 9

Radical Ideas

From what little I have seen of the fossil World and Natural History, I think the connection or analogy between the Creatures of the former and present World excepting as to size, much greater than is generally supposed.

Mary Anning

The Industrial Revolution in the late eighteenth and early nineteenth centuries was a boon to geologists. Canals dug to transport coal across England and stone quarried for building material revealed a bounty of fossils. William Smith was a surveyor who traveled around England studying rocks to find the best coal seams and places to dig canals. He saw that sedimentary rocks occurred in sequences and that different layers in those sequences contained different fossils. He realized he could use fossils to identify strata of the same age that were exposed in different parts of the country. William

Smith created a detailed map of the strata of England, Wales, and part of Scotland and published it in 1815. His map showed that the rocks exposed in the cliffs near Lyme Regis stretched northeast

William Smith hand-colored his unique map—the first-ever detailed geological map of a country. Each color represents a different rock type, such as green for chalk and blue for limestone. The finished map was made up of fifteen sections and measured 8½ x 6 feet. Approximately 400 copies were printed but only a few remain.

across England and up to the Yorkshire coast. Since those rocks contained the fossils of marine animals, geologists knew that what is now the southeast of England must once have been covered by the sea. Scientists had long theorized about the processes that created the earth's crust. Some thought rocks had formed from minerals suspended in water that covered the earth. Others thought that heat at the center of the earth had created the continents. James Hutton believed that changes in the earth's crust were caused by ongoing processes that had acted in the past and were continuing in the present. But most of these discussions took place among scientists alone; it wasn't until the Scottish geologist Charles Lyell published a three-volume book in 1830 titled *Principles of Geology: Being an Attempt to Explain the Former Changes of the Earth's Surface* that the general public was introduced to geological principles. By that time steam-powered printing presses had made book production faster and cheaper, and books were more readily available to ordinary people. Lyell's *Principles of Geology* was well written and popular; it helped to spread the theory of an ancient earth that had changed over millions of years.

While Charles Lyell conveyed scientific information to the public with his words, Henry De La Beche used drawings. The fossils that Mary Anning found were the remains of animals that had never been seen alive, but that didn't stop Henry from imagining what they looked like. In 1830, he painted a picture of a Jurassic

In Henry De La Beche's lively Jurassic scene a crocodile watches from land as an ichthyosaur bites the neck of a terrified, defecating plesiosaur and pterodactyls fly above them. Henry sold prints of his Duria Antiquior *to raise money for Mary Anning; it is one of the earliest examples of paleoart.*

sea filled with living versions of Mary's fossils and titled it *Duria Antiquior* (or *More Ancient Dorset*). Still, most people could not accept that frightening animals like the ones in his painting had once swum in a sea covering much of England.

Reluctant to accept that whole species had simply disappeared from the earth, some people suggested that they were just hiding. But by 1812, Georges Cuvier had already identified more than forty extinct animals; it was unlikely they were *all* hiding in deep ocean caves or on remote islands. In a footnote from a book they published in 1822, William Conybeare and William Phillips noted that since more than two hundred species of ammonite, some of which were over three feet wide and all of which could float, had been identified from fossil finds, they couldn't all be hiding. And since big ichthyosaurs and plesiosaurs had to surface to breathe air, surely sailors would have spotted one if they still existed. Some scholars and clergymen suggested that the missing animals had all been drowned in a worldwide flood, but a flood would have drowned people, too, and no human fossils were found in the rocks.

By 1837, the English naturalist Charles Darwin was formulating his own ideas about missing species. He had long been interested in geology, writing to his sister in 1832 that nothing could compare "to finding a fine group of fossil bones, which tell their story of former times with almost a living tongue." In 1859, after years spent gathering information and data, Darwin published his theory that animals evolved over time through a process he called natural selection. He believed that because more individuals of a species are born than can survive (given the earth's limited resources), there was a constant struggle for survival. Any animal with physical variations that gave it an advantage—such as an extra-long neck that allowed it to reach fruit higher in the trees than others of its species could reach—had a better chance of thriving and successfully

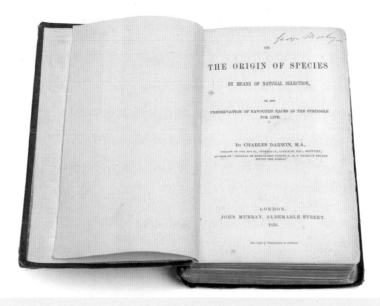

Charles Darwin's famous book, On the Origin of Species, *printed in 1859.*

reproducing. It had been "naturally selected." Darwin's famous book was titled *On the Origin of Species by Means of Natural Selection, or the Preservation of Favoured Races in the Struggle for Life.*

Some clergymen were outraged by these new theories that seemed to contradict the Church's teachings about the origins of life on earth. Geologists who were also clergymen, such as William Buckland and William Conybeare, struggled to fit their scientific discoveries into their religious beliefs.

Mary Anning attended church, studied the Bible, and copied religious texts into a journal called a commonplace book. How did she reconcile her religious beliefs with the latest geological theories about the age of the earth, extinction, and evolution? We don't know, because she left us few clues. We can imagine that she discussed new theories with friends such as William Buckland and Henry

De La Beche. She must have been interested in the topic, because she copied out William Conybeare and William Phillips's footnote in which they discussed whether fossil species were extinct or just hidden. And when a friend wrote to her in 1844 describing lectures she had attended, Mary responded that the connections between "creatures of the former and present World" must be greater than most people thought. But that's all we know about her thoughts on the topic of the earth's ancient history. She never had the opportunity to read Charles Darwin's book, because she died before it was published.

Geologists such as Adam Sedgwick, Charles Lyell, Roderick Murchison, and Richard Owen did not accept Darwin's theory that animals evolved over time through natural selection. The geological record was too imperfect: strata had

Charles Darwin was a keen geologist as well as a naturalist. He was fascinated by the geology of the places he visited on his famous journey around the world, and he collected rocks and fossils as well as made many observations in his notebooks.

been eroded, leaving gaps representing millions of years. The fossils from those rocks, and the clues they gave about evolution, were therefore missing.

But exposed in the ninety-five-mile stretch of coast extending east and west of Lyme Regis is an almost complete record of strata from three geologic time periods—the Triassic, Jurassic, and Cretaceous. The fossils Mary Anning found in some of those rocks, so unlike any living animals, provided key evidence of extinction and helped geologists build a picture of a complex prehistoric world where the strong preyed on the weak and the best-adapted animals survived.

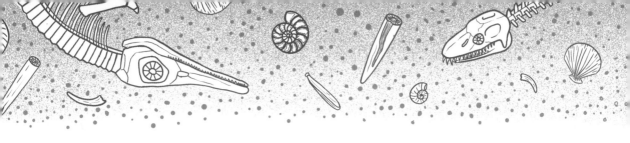

CHAPTER 10

Legacy

[Mary Anning] . . . though not placed among even the easier classes of society, but who had to earn her daily bread by her labour, yet contributed by her talents and untiring researches in no small degree to our knowledge of the great Enalio-saurians [extinct reptiles], and other forms of organic life.

Sir Henry De La Beche, 1848

Mary Anning saved money whenever she could, and by the time she was thirty-six years old she had two hundred pounds as insurance against future hard times. She decided to invest the money, but unfortunately the man she chose to assist her died and her savings disappeared. News of Mary's misfortune spread, and the men of science who had done little to help her in the past decided to help her now. Members of the British Society for the Advancement of

Science collected money, and the British government added more to the fund until there was enough to give Mary a yearly pension of twenty-five pounds for the rest of her life. This was an income Mary could depend on, and with the extra money from the sale of her fossils, she could live comfortably.

In October 1842, Mary's mother, Molly, died. Mary was forty-three and alone for the first time in her life—she had never married. A husband would probably have expected her to give up fossil hunting because spending time alone on the beach with other men was deemed inappropriate for a married woman. Caring for children and doing household chores such as fetching water from the well, washing laundry by hand, shopping, cooking, and cleaning would have left no time for preparing fossils. Marriage might have solved some of Mary's financial problems, but it would have ended her independence and her career.

After her mother's death all that greeted Mary after a long, hard day on the beach was a cold, empty house. Her geologist friends did not visit her as often as they once had, and she had not found any exceptional fossils for several years—but in July 1844 she sold a fine ichthyosaur to two elegant gentlemen who entered her shop. Mary's customers were King Frederick Augustus II of Saxony and his personal physician, Dr. Carl Gustav Carus. She probably did not recognize the king, who was traveling without the usual pomp and ceremony of a royal visit, but Mary must have noticed his German accent. When she wrote her name and address in Dr. Carus's pocket book, she added these words, "I am well known throughout the whole of Europe." By that time, geologists in Europe and America knew of Mary's skill at fossil collection and preparation, and she was justifiably proud of her accomplishments.

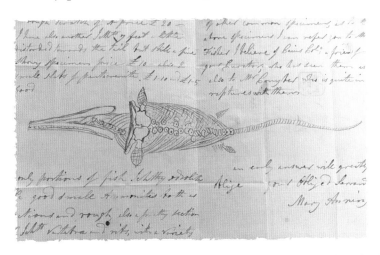

Mary Anning included this drawing, which she called a "rough scratch," in a letter she wrote to geologist Adam Sedgwick in 1843. She hoped he would buy the fossil from her for the price of £20.

In 1845, when she was only forty-six years old, Mary Anning's health failed her. For the first time in her life she didn't have the strength and energy for the physically demanding work of fossil hunting. She had breast cancer. Any diagnosis of cancer was a death sentence in nineteenth-century England; doctors could do little to help their patients. Surgery was performed without anesthetics or antibiotics, and the patient was likely to die of shock or infection.

All Mary's doctor could do was give her a liquid medicine called laudanum to ease her pain.

Despite her illness, Mary went down to the beach—her special place—whenever she could. On the beach she had overcome all the obstacles that tried to defeat her—the sea that wanted to steal her treasures, the rocks that wouldn't release them, and her rivals, the other fossil hunters. On the beach she had matched learned men in strength, skill, and intellect. On the beach she had not been Mary Anning, unmarried carpenter's daughter, but Mary Anning, expert fossil hunter and self-taught paleontologist.

Mary could not overcome her final challenge. She died in March 1847 and was buried in the graveyard at St. Michael's Church just above the cliffs where she had found so many fossils. In the church-yard today is a simple gray gravestone speckled with lichen and carved with the names of Mary and her brother, Joseph. A few years after her death, Mary's friends raised money for a stained-glass win-dow to be placed in St. Michael's Church in her memory.

The year after Mary's death, her old friend Henry De La Beche was knighted by Queen Victoria and also became the president of the Geological Society, which by that time had almost nine hun-dred male members (women were still not allowed to join). In his first speech to the Society as its president, Sir Henry remembered prominent members who had died in the previous year. And then he talked about Mary. Even though she had not been a member, he spoke of her early life and reminded everyone of her contributions to science, including her skill at reassembling fossil skeletons:

> *There are those among us in this room who know well how to appreciate the skill she employed . . . in developing the remains of the many fine skeletons of Ichthyosauri and Plesiosauri, which without her care would never have been presented to comparative anatomists in the uninjured form so desirable for examination.*

Indeed, Mary's fossils had been the foundation for pioneering work on the history of life on earth. In praising her to this large group of distinguished geologists and learned men, Sir Henry De La Beche was, at last, giving Mary Anning public recognition for her contributions to science.

Every summer the narrow streets of Lyme Regis teem with tourists on vacation. Many visit the museum close to the site of Mary's first home, where they learn about her life and accomplishments. Some go to her gravestone at St. Michael's Church to pay their respects, while others follow in her footsteps on the foreshore, hunting for fossils on the slippery seaweed-covered rock ledges and in the sticky mud beneath the cliffs of Black Ven. Mary's two homes are gone now, and the chapel she once attended is a fossil museum. But just down the street, set into an ancient stone wall, is the old wooden post box where she mailed letters to her friends.

Many of the extraordinary fossils Mary found have been lost—some were misplaced by the museums that owned them and some were destroyed by bombs during World War II. But others can be seen in museums in the United Kingdom, the United States, and Europe. The first ichthyosaur that Joseph and Mary found is displayed at the Natural History Museum in London in a case with another of Mary's huge ichthyosaurs.

After her death, Mary's nephew sold her drawings, letters, notebooks, and papers to the Earl of Enniskillen. The earl offered them to the geologist Richard Owen, writing, "It will amuse you to scan them over, and do as you please with them." In Victorian England women could not vote, study at university, hold political office, or do professional work. Women were thought capable only of managing a home, bearing children, or doing menial labor; they were not thought capable of intellectual work. Because women were not thought of as serious scientists, Mary's important papers were treated carelessly by men such as the Earl of Enniskillen. All we have left are a few surviving letters she wrote to friends and customers, her commonplace book, and a little of her writing.

But still, more than one hundred and seventy years after Mary's death, her name is much more widely known than any of the men she called "big wigs." While William Buckland, Henry De La Beche, and William Conybeare are remembered mostly by scholars of the

William Buckland giving a lecture at Oxford University in 1825. The attendees are all men — women were not allowed to attend university at the time. William Buckland did not believe that women could be serious scientists, even though both his wife and Mary Anning helped him in his work.

history of geology, Mary Anning is celebrated worldwide by students, geologists, and ordinary people. She is now recognized as a serious scientist—in 1999, the Palaeontological Association named an award after her, and in 2010, the Royal Society named her as one of the ten most influential women in British science history. She also now has several fossils named after her, including a new species of ichthyosaur—*Ichthyosaurus anningae*. And she has inspired many authors and moviemakers to document her life.

Mary Anning's legacy lies not only in the fossils she found and the contributions she made to science, but also in the example

she set for women to follow. Unwilling to be limited by English customs of the time, Mary pursued fossil hunting with dogged determination. Intelligent, curious, persistent, and tough, she built an extraordinary career. She will forever be remembered for changing how we understand the history of life on earth.

This display case in the Natural History Museum in London holds a twenty-foot-long Ichthyosaurus platyodon *(now renamed* Temnodontosaurus platyodon*) found by Mary Anning. In the lower left is the ichthyosaur found by Mary and her brother, Joseph, that was the first to be carefully studied by scientists. At the bottom of the case is a line of vertebrae from another big ichthyosaur.*

fibrous spathose conical shell, divided...
separate cells or cha...

+ though an ignorance of the true nature of the mollu...
inhabiting the chambered univalves has led him to...
several erroneous opinion with regard to the exact man...
formation. He observes that the concave septa in the...
conical shell, as having sustained no pressure were conse...
as siphuncle, and suggests that the animal lived in its out...
ber: he also considers the shell as having sustained no...
and proves this from the vestiges of its laminæ cons...
which he compares to that of the Oyster. yet Platt does no...
with Dr Hook, that the siphuncle extends through al...
—mbers, and gives rather unsatisfactory account of the m...
in which the animal is, according to his hypothesis,
the aperture of its first chamber without separating of...
siphuncle and to assume a figure which may permit ...
on the bottom of the sea, and to drag its shell with it. He...
that the animal both on its return and in its progr...
the whole guard by two flaps or sides of its mantle, as a...
does a small branch of a tree, and that in so doing it dep...
enction the lamelæ which form the guard (in a man...
similar to that in which the Cypraea increases its...
the sulcus; which may be observed traversing the su...
the Belemnite longitudinally he considers as ind...
the interval in which the two flaps of the mantle m...
have met in thus clasping the guard.
As the chambered portion of the Belemnite is so close...
—gous to the shell of the nautilus,— Walch, Parkins...
Lamarck agree in the opinion that like that shell
to aid the buoyancy of its inhabitant...

AUTHOR'S NOTE

In my undergraduate days, the early geologists we read about were all men. I didn't know anything about Mary Anning until 2014, when what would have been her 215th birthday was celebrated in a Google Doodle. I discovered that although Mary had found and prepared some of England's most important fossils, she received little professional recognition during her lifetime. If she'd been a privileged, educated man, like the early geologists who took advantage of her knowledge and expertise, she would certainly have received more accolades for her work. But she was poor, uneducated, and a woman, which made her easy to overlook. When I learned those basic facts, I knew I had to write this book. Although I'd given up geology as soon as I graduated (at the time there weren't many career options for female geologists), I was delighted that researching this extraordinary woman allowed me to once again immerse myself in geological topics.

Digging for facts about Mary Anning is a lot like digging for fossils—it requires patience and is often unsuccessful. Even what should be straightforward information, such as Mary's age when she found her first famous ichthyosaur fossil, is often shrouded in mystery. Was she eleven, twelve, or thirteen? Different authors have reached different conclusions. One of my biggest frustrations was having so little information on Mary's thoughts about her life and on how her fossil finds affected her religious beliefs. The little we do know comes from the recollections of other people or from hints in those few of her letters that have survived to the present day. Anna Maria Pinney, one of Mary's upper-class women friends, wrote brief journal entries about their fossil-collecting exploits and included her opinions on Mary's life. In one entry, she described Mary as suffering for eight years from a mysterious physical and mental illness caused by someone's "treachery." Unfortunately, she didn't explain the illness or the treachery, so we are left to guess. Anna Maria depicted Mary as a complicated person—religious (like Anna Maria herself), proud, sometimes rude to people Anna Maria thought she should have respected, and yet kind, generous, and affectionate too. Anna Maria called Mary an "ascetic"—a person who led an austere, simple life and denied herself material pleasures—although we don't know if that was by choice or from lack of money.

I imagine Mary as an intelligent, curious, practical individual, not intimidated by those better educated and wealthier than she was, but resentful that her opportunities were limited by her gender and social status. I expect she'd be pleased to know that now she is much more famous outside of geological circles than the men with whom she worked. She'd probably be astonished that a short letter she wrote to William Buckland when she was twenty-nine years old sold at auction in 2020 to a private collector for over $130,000.

She'd be surprised, and gratified, to know that an eleven-year-old girl, Evie Swire, began a campaign called "Mary Anning Rocks" to raise money to erect a statue of her in Lyme Regis. I'm certain she would be delighted that, over 170 years after her death, some of her fossils are still on display in world-class museums and are now attributed to her. Finally, Mary Anning is receiving the recognition she deserves.

— *Cheryl Blackford*

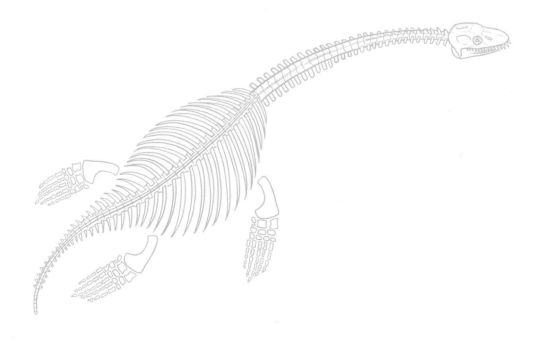

ACKNOWLEDGMENTS

Many, many people helped me as I wrote this book, and I'm grateful to every one of them.

My thanks to:

Hannah Lowery (Bristol University library); Anna Butler (Dorset County Museum); Hillary Ketchum and Kate Diston (Oxford Museum of Natural History); Matt Riley, Sarah Wallace Johnson, and Sandra Freshney (Sedgwick Museum of Earth Sciences, Cambridge); Mike Day, Hellen Pethers, and Mark Graham (Natural History Museum, London); Richard Bull and David Tucker (Lyme Regis Museum, Lyme Regis); and Jessica Lippincott (Wyoming Dinosaur Center) for their expert advice and assistance.

Sally Abraham for her translation skills and Sir Crispin Tickell for his assistance with one of Mary's "scratches."

Paddy Howe—despite his expert guidance, I failed miserably at finding fossils on Mary's beaches. She would have been appalled.

Nick Gardner, Joschua Knüppe, Peter Montgomery, John Sibbick, Tom Sermon, and Esther van Hulsen for their gorgeous photos and artwork, and Mark Witton for creating the evocative *"Temnodontosaurus* Fall" illustration at the beginning of the book.

Stephanie Son for the fabulous cover, Ellen Duda for the interior design and beautiful line art throughout the book, and Ed DuRose, who patiently enhanced the lovely old drawings and my poor photos to make them suitable for publication.

My writing sisters—Julie Evans, Patti Kester, Joy Klaas, Yvonne Pearson, Shireen Rahnema, Jackie Rust, Catherine Urdahl, and Elizabeth Verdick—your love and support sustain me. My early readers—Tom Goodhue, Jasper Griffin, Molly Beth Griffin, Dr. Dean Lomax, and Carrie Pomeroy—your thoughtful comments made this a better book.

My editor, Ann Rider, and the rest of the team at Houghton Mifflin Harcourt Books for Young Readers—Susan Bishansky, Celeste Knudsen, Harriet Low, Mary Magrisso, Alison Miller, and Erika West—who worked their magic and turned my manuscript into a beautiful book.

Mum and Dad for encouraging me to study geology at a time when not many women did. David, for driving me hundreds of miles from museum to museum and waiting patiently while I was engrossed in fossils and documents—I couldn't have done this without him. If I've forgotten anyone, I'm sorry, and if there are any mistakes in this book, they are mine and mine alone.

TIMELINE

1796 — Richard and Molly Anning have a son they name Joseph.

1799 — Richard and Molly Anning have a daughter they name Mary.

1803 — Britain declares war on France. The Napoleonic Wars last twelve years and have a devastating social and economic impact in Britain, France, and other European countries.

1804 — Dr. James Parkinson publishes *Organic Remains of a Former World*, the first book to give scientific information about fossils.

1807 — The Geological Society of London is created by thirteen men over dinner.

1807 — The British Parliament passes an act to abolish the slave trade (carrying captives overseas by ship). Slavery is not abolished in England until 1833.

1809 — The British naturalist Charles Darwin is born.

1810 — Richard Anning dies from a combination of a fall and illness.

1811 — Joseph Anning finds an ichthyosaur skull later determined to be the species *Ichthyosaurus platyodon*.

1812 — Mary Anning finds the body of the *Ichthyosaurus platyodon* (later renamed *Temnodontosaurus platyodon*). The Annings' fossil was the first ichthyosaur to be carefully studied by scientists. It is now displayed at the Natural History Museum in London.

1812 — On June 18, the United States declares war on Britain.

1814 — The British engineer and inventor George Stephenson designs the first steam engine.

1815 — The war between the United States and Britain ends.

1815 — The surveyor William Smith publishes a map of the strata of England, Wales, and part of Scotland. It was the first detailed geological map of a country.

1818 — William Buckland becomes the first reader (professor) in geology at Oxford University.

1823 — Mary Anning finds the first complete plesiosaur fossil (*Plesiosaurus giganteus*). Scientists at the time thought this was her most important fossil. Today it is displayed at the Natural History Museum in London.

1824 — William Buckland is the first geologist to formally describe a dinosaur—*Megalosaurus*. (The name *dinosaur* has not yet been invented.)

1824 — The British doctor and geologist Gideon Mantell publishes the second paper on a dinosaur (*Iguanodon*).

1824 — Mary Anning suspects bezoar stones are actually fossilized feces.

1825 — The Stockton and Darlington Railroad (the first to use steam locomotives in Britain) opens.

1828 — Mary Anning discovers the first British pterosaur, *Pterodactylus macronyx* (now known as *Dimorphodon macronyx*). The Natural History Museum in London holds the fossil.

1829 — Mary Anning finds the first squaloraja fossil (*Squaloraja polyspondyla*), but the tail is missing. Most of the squaloraja fossil was destroyed during World War II, but the tail is now held in the Philpot Collection at the Oxford University Museum of Natural History.

1830 — Mary Anning finds a beautiful plesiosaur fossil—*Plesiosaurus macrocephalus*. The fossil is displayed at the Natural History Museum in London.

1830 — Charles Lyell publishes the first edition of his popular book *Principles of Geology*. Charles Darwin takes the book with him on his voyage on the *Beagle*.

1831–36 — Charles Darwin travels overseas on the *Beagle*. He gathers information and conducts scientific studies that will help him formulate his theories of evolution and natural selection.

1833 — Mary Anning's dog, Tray, is killed in a rockfall.

1841 — Louis Agassiz names a fossil fish *Acrodus anningiae* after Mary Anning.

1842 — Richard Owen gives the name *Dinosauria* to land reptiles that first appeared in the Triassic era more than 230 million years ago.

1842 — Molly Anning, Mary's mother, dies.

1844 — Louis Agassiz names another fossil fish, *Belenostomus anningiae*, after Mary Anning.

1847 — Mary Anning dies on March 9.

1849 — Joseph Anning dies.

1859 — Charles Darwin publishes his famous book *On the Origin of Species by Means of Natural Selection, or The Preservation of Favoured Races in the Struggle for Life.*

1869 — Nine women become the first female students to attend a university in Britain.

1919 — Women are finally allowed to join the Geological Society of London.

1999 — The Palaeontological Association names an award after Mary Anning.

2010 — The Royal Society includes Mary Anning in a list of the most influential women in the history of British science.

2015 — Dr. Dean Lomax and Professor Judy Massare identify a new species of ichthyosaur and name it *Ichthyosaurus anningae* after Mary Anning.

2020 — A drilling location on Mars is named after Mary Anning. A nearby ChemCam (chemistry and camera) target is named after her dog, Tray.

GLOSSARY

AMMONITE (am-eh-nite): Extinct marine molluscs with a coiled external shell. Ammonites belonged to a class of animals called cephalopods and are related to modern squid and octopi. Ammonites lived on the earth for 140 million years during the Jurassic and Cretaceous periods.

ANATOMY (an-at-uh-me): The body structure of an animal. A person who studies anatomy is an anatomist.

BELEMNITE (bel-em-nite): Extinct marine molluscs with a long, slender internal skeleton. Belemnites belonged to a class of animals called cephalopods and are related to modern squid and octopi. Belemnites lived on earth from about 200 to 66 million years ago during the Jurassic and Cretaceous periods.

CHISEL (chih-zel): A metal tool with a sharp edge used to carve wood, stone, or metal.

COPROLITE (kop-reh-lite): Fossilized feces.

CRETACEOUS (kreh-tay-shus): A geological time period that stretched from about 145 to 66 million years ago. Dinosaurs (excluding birds) and many other species became extinct at the end of the Cretaceous period.

CRINOID (cry-noid): Crinoids, or sea lilies, are related to sea urchins and starfish. Their stems, formed from columns of hard plates, are topped with a cup-shaped body and a central mouth sur-rounded by five branching feathery arms. Crinoids first appeared about 300 million years ago, and some species still exist today.

CRUST (krust): The earth's crust is the layer of rock on the earth's exterior. The crust floats on the mantle (the layer of rock above the core).

CURIOSITIES (cure-ee-oss-ih-tees): Unusual or odd objects, some-times kept in a collection. Lyme Regis residents often called fossils "curiosities" or "curies."

DEBT (det): Something, such as money, that is owed to someone. A person who must repay a debt is called a debtor.

DEPOSITION (dep-ih-zi-shen): The geological process in which sediments (such as sand and mud) are laid down on land, in rivers and lakes, or beneath the sea. These sediments may build up in layers.

DIGIT (dih-jiht): A finger, thumb, or toe.

DINOSAUR (die-neh-sore): Terrestrial, egg-laying reptiles. Non-avian dinosaurs (dinosaurs that are not birds) lived on earth from about 230 to 66 million years ago. Since scientists now believe that birds are feathered dinosaurs, not all dinosaurs are extinct.

DORSAL (dor-suhl): Something on, or part of, an animal's back, such as a dorsal fin.

EROSION (ih-roh-zhen): The geological process in which soil, sand, mud, and rock is worn away by the action of wind, water, or ice and the resulting material is carried away.

EVOLUTION (ehv-eh-loo-shun): The gradual change in the characteristics of a species by the process of natural selection over many generations. The species are said to "evolve."

EXTINCT (ehk-stinkt): No longer existing. A species that no longer exists is said to be extinct.

FOSSIL (fah-sill): The preserved remains of ancient organisms. Fossils can be the preserved hard parts of animals, such as bones or teeth, or the traces of animals, such as footprints, burrows, or feces.

GENUS (jee-nehs): A category of biological classification. Genus and species—the lowest levels of the classification—make up an animal's name. A genus can be subdivided into one or more species. Mary Anning's first ichthyosaur was named *Ichthyosaurus platyodon*; *Ichthyosaurus* was the genus. This fossil has since been reclassified and is now known as *Temnodontosaurus platyodon*. *Ichthyosaurus* and *Temnodontosaurus* are two different genuses of ichthyosaur.

ICHTHYOSAUR (ihk-thee-eh-sore): Extinct, air-breathing, carnivorous marine reptiles that lived from 248 to 90 million years ago during the Triassic, Jurassic, and Cretaceous periods.

JURASSIC (jer-as-ihk): A geological time period that stretched from about 200 to 145 million years ago. The Jurassic is divided into Upper, Middle, and Lower Jurassic series of rock formations. The limestones and shales where Mary Anning found many of her fossils belong to the Blue Lias formation of the Upper Triassic and Lower Jurassic (formed 200 to 195 million years ago).

LIMESTONE (lime-stone): Sedimentary rock usually formed in warm, shallow water from shells, coral, algae, and animal waste. Gray limestones, like those near Lyme Regis, have clay in them.

MARINE (meh-reen): Something associated with or living in the sea.

MARL (marl): A soft, crumbly sedimentary rock that is a lime-rich mudstone.

MATRIX (may-trihx): In geology, matrix is the natural material in which a fossil or a crystal is embedded.

MUDSTONE (mud-stone): A dark gray sedimentary rock formed from hardened mud.

PALEOART (pay-lee-oh-art): Artistic representations recreating prehistoric life and habitats. *Duria Antiquior* by Henry De La Beche is an early example of paleoart.

PALEONTOLOGIST (pay-lee-on-tol-uh-jist): A geologist who collects and studies fossils is called a paleontologist.

PETRIFY (peh-trih-fy): To turn to stone.

PLESIOSAUR (ple-see-eh-sore): Extinct, air-breathing, carnivorous marine reptiles that lived from about 203 to 66 million years ago during the late Triassic, Jurassic, and Cretaceous periods.

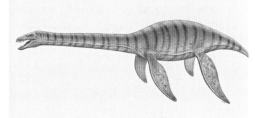

PTEROSAUR (ter-ah-sore): Extinct, carnivorous, warm-blooded, egg-laying, flying reptiles that lived from 228 to 66 million years ago. Pterosaurs were the first flying vertebrates on earth; some lived in coastal areas while others lived in forests and swamps. *Pterodactylus* is one genus of pterosaur; *Dimorphodon* is another.

SANDSTONE (sand-stone): A sedimentary rock formed from sand-grain-size minerals, such as quartz, cemented together. Sandstone can be pink, red, orange, yellow, white, brown, gray, and even black.

SEDIMENT (seh-dih-ment): Eroded material, such as sand or silt, carried away by wind, water, or ice and deposited elsewhere. Rocks formed from this type of material are called sedimentary rocks.

SHALE (shayl): A fine-grained sedimentary rock formed from clay, mud, or silt. Shale can be split into thin layers.

SPECIES (spee-shees): A category of biological classification. Members of a species share common characteristics. Genus and species—the lowest levels of the classification—make up an animal's name. A genus is subdivided into different species. Example: In *Plesiosaurus macrocephalus* the genus is *Plesiosaurus* and the species is *macrocephalus*.

SQUALORAJA (skwah-ler-ay-jeh): Fish with a skeleton made from cartilage that lived about 200 million years ago during the Lower Jurassic period.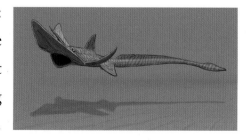

Squaloraja had flat bodies like those of stingrays, large eyes, and a long snout.

STRATA (strah-teh): Distinctive layers of rock.

TERRESTRIAL (ter-est-ri-uhl): Associated with or living on land.

TIDE (tide): The rise and fall of sea level caused by the moon's or the sun's gravitational pull and the earth's rotation. High tide is when the sea is closest to the shore; low tide is when the sea is farthest away from the shore.

TRIASSIC (tri-ass-ihk): A geological time period that stretched from about 250 to 200 million years ago. The first true mammals and the first flying vertebrates (pterosaurs) evolved during this period. The Triassic period was followed by the Jurassic period.

VERTEBRA (ver-teh-bruh): One of the bones in a series that form the backbone (spine) of an animal. The plural of *vertebra* is *vertebrae*. An animal with a backbone is called a *vertebrate*.

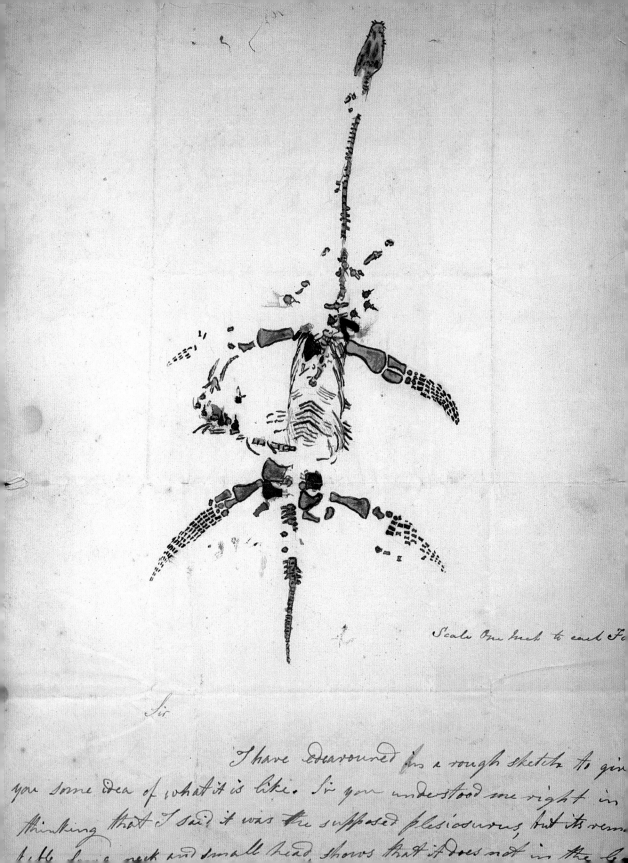

Scale One Inch to each Fo

Sir

I have endeavoured for a rough sketch to give
you some idea of what it is like. Sir you understood me right in
thinking that I said it was the supposed plesiosaurus, but its very
little long neck and small head, shows that it does not in the le

WHERE TO SEE MARY ANNING'S FOSSILS

Mary Anning sold her fossils to private collectors and institutions. Unfortunately, we don't have a good record of how many of Mary's fossils still exist; some have been lost, some were destroyed by bombs during World War II, and some might be stored in collections but without proof that they were found by Mary.

You can see some of Mary's fossils, or exhibitions about Mary, at the following places:

Bristol Museum and Art Gallery, Bristol, England

British Geological Survey, Nottingham, England

Dorset County Museum, Dorchester, England

Lyme Regis Museum, Lyme Regis, England

Muséum National d'Histoire Naturelle, Paris, France

Natural History Museum, London, England
(Excellent fossils are displayed in the museum's marine reptiles gallery.)

Oxford University Museum of Natural History, Oxford, England

Sedgwick Museum of Earth Sciences, Cambridge, England

SOURCE QUOTES

Chapter 1. Crocodile or Sea Monster?

"*A few days ago, immediately after the late high tide*": Howe et al., *Ichthyosaurs*, p. 9.

Chapter 2. Learning on the Beach

"*They was all three stricken by the Lightning*": Lang, "Mary Anning's Escape from Lightning," p. 91.

Chapter 3. Not a Lady

"*It is certainly uncommon*": Hack, *Geological Sketches and Glimpses of the Ancient Earth*, p. 302.

"*I do so enjoy*": Lang, "Three Letters by Mary Anning," p. 169.

"*I believe the best thing*": Ibid., p. 170.

"*They were great fossilists*": Edmonds, "The Fossil Collection of the Misses Philpot," p. 47.

"*She has been noticed by all the cleverest men*": Lang, "Mary Anning and Anna Maria Pinney," p. 147.

Chapter 4. Geological Mysteries

"*The extraordinary thing in this young woman*": Emling, *The Fossil Hunter*, p. 89.

"*I am going to sell my collection*": Ibid., p. 261.

"*As I am a widow woman*": Mary Anning Sr. (Molly Anning), letter, Natural History Museum, London.

"*This persevering female*": Torrens, "Mary Anning of Lyme," p. 263.

"*[Mary] says the world has used her ill*": Lang, "Mary Anning and Anna Maria Pinney," p. 147.

Chapter 5. A Second Sea Monster

"*It is large and heavy*": Mary Anning, letter, Natural History, Museum London.

"*To the head of the lizard*": Buckland, *Geology and Mineralogy Considered*, p. 202.

Chapter 6. A New Home

"*A plain unpretending little shop*": Pierce, *Jurassic Mary*, p. 98.

"*what a sense of horror we have gone through at Lyme*": Grant, *A Memoir of Miss Frances Augusta Bell*, p. 132.

"*She would serve us with the sweetest temper*": Ibid.

Chapter 7. More Important Fossils

"*A monster resembling nothing*": Buckland (from Cuvier), "On the Discovery of a New Species of Pterodactyle," p. 217.

"*within the ribs*": Buckland, "On the Discovery of Coprolites," p. 224.

"*A head like a pair of scissors*": Taylor, "Saleswoman to a New Science," p. 136.

Chapter 8. From Excitement to Heartache

"*It is without exception*": Lang, "Mary Anning and the Pioneer Geologists," p. 155.

"*With the kind assistance of Miss Anning*": Hawkins, *Memoirs of Ichthyosauri*, p. 11.

"*He makes things as he imagines*": Lang, "Three Letters by Mary Anning," p. 171.

"*My Dear Madam*": Ibid.

Chapter 9. Radical Ideas

"*From what little I have seen of the fossil World*": Pierce, *Jurassic Mary*, p. 51.

"*to finding a fine group*": Maddox, *Reading the Rocks*, p. 127.

Chapter 10. Legacy

"*though not placed among*": Lang, "Mary Anning and the Pioneer Geologists of Lyme," p. 162.

"*I am well known*": Carus, *King of Saxony's Journey*, p. 197.

"*there are those among us*": Ibid.

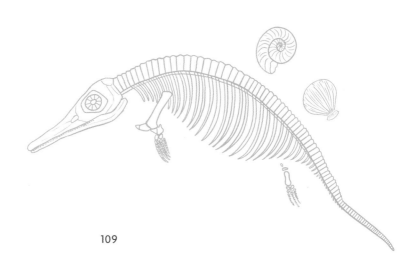

BIBLIOGRAPHY

Ackermann, Rudolph. *The Repository of Arts, Literature, Commerce, Manufactures, Fashions and Politics*, vol. 9, London: L. Harrison, 1810.

Brown, H. Rowland. *The Beauties of Lyme Regis, Charmouth, the Land-Slip and Their Vicinities; Topographically and Historically Considered*. Lyme Regis: Daniel Dunster, 1857.

Buckland, William. *Vindiciae Geologicae, or The Connexion of Religion with Geology Explained*. Oxford: Oxford University Press, 1820.

———. "On the Discovery of a New Species of Pterodactyle in the Lias at Lyme Regis." *Transactions of the Geological Society*, series 2, vol. 3 (1835), pp. 217–22.

———. "On the Discovery of Coprolites, or Fossil Faeces, in the Lias at Lyme Regis, and in other formations." *Transactions of the Geological Society*, series 2, vol. 3 (1835), pp. 223–36.

———. *Geology and Mineralogy Considered with Reference to Natural Theology*. London: William Pickering, 1836.

Cadbury, Deborah. *The Dinosaur Hunters*. London: Fourth Estate, 2000.

Carus, Dr. C. G. *King of Saxony's Journey Through England and Scotland in the Year 1844*. London: Chapman and Hall, 1846.

Conybeare, Rev. W. D. "On the Discovery of an Almost Perfect Skeleton of the Plesiosaurus." *Transactions of the Geological Society*, series 2, vol. 1 (1822), pp. 381–87.

Conybeare, Rev. W. D., and William Philips. "Outlines of the Geology of England and Wales with an Introductory Compendium of the General Principles of That Science and Comparative Views of the Structure of Foreign Countries." London: William Phillips, 1822, p ix.

Edmonds, J. M. "The Fossil Collection of the Misses Philpot of Lyme Regis." *Proceedings of the Dorset Natural History and Archaeological Society*, vol. 98, (1977), pp. 43–48.

Emling, Shelley. *The Fossil Hunter*. New York: Palgrave Macmillan, 2009.

Fowles, John. *A Short History of Lyme Regis*. Wimborne, UK: Dovecote Press, 1991.

Goodhue, Thomas W. *Curious Bones: Mary Anning and the Birth of Paleontology*. Greensboro, NC: Morgan Reynolds, 2002.

———. *Fossil Hunter: The Life and Times of Mary Anning*. Washington, DC: Academica Press, 2004.

Gordon, Mrs. *The Life and Correspondence of William Buckland*, DD, F.R.S. London: John Murray, 1894.

Gould, Stephen Jay, and Rosamund Wolf Purcell. *Finders, Keepers: Eight Collectors*. New York: Norton, 1992.

Grant, Rev. Johnson. *A Memoir of Miss Frances Augusta Bell*. London: Hatchard and Son, 1827.

Hack, Maria. *Geological Sketches and Glimpses of the Ancient Earth*. London: Harvey and Darton, 1822.

Hawkins, Thomas. *Memoirs of Ichthyosauri and Plesiosauri Extinct Monsters of the Ancient Earth*. London: Relfe and Fletcher, 1834.

———. *The Book of the Great Sea Dragons, Ichthyosauri and Plesiosauri*. London: William Pickering, 1840.

Home, Everard. "Some Account of the Fossil Remains of an Animal More Nearly Allied to Fishes Than Any of the Other Classes of Animals." *Philosophical Transactions of the Royal Society*, 1814, pp. 571–77.

———. "An Account of the Fossil Skeleton of the Proteo-Saurus." *Philosophical Transactions of the Royal Society*, 1819, pp. 209–11.

———. "Reasons for Giving the Name Proteo-Saurus to the Fossil Skeleton Which Has Been Described." *Philosophical Transactions of the Royal Society* (1819), pp. 212–16.

Howe S. R., T. Sharpe, and H. S. Torrens. *Ichthyosaurs: A History of Fossil "Sea Dragons."* Cardiff, Wales: National Museums and Galleries of Wales, 1981.

Lang, W. D. "Mary Anning (1799–1847) and the Pioneer Geologists of Lyme." *Proceedings of the Dorset Natural History and Archaeological Society*, vol. 60 (1939), pp. 142–64.

———. "Three Letters by Mary Anning, 'Fossilist' of Lyme." *Proceedings of the Dorset Natural History and Archaeological Society*, vol. 66 (1945), pp. 169–73.

———. "More About Mary Anning, including a Newly Found Letter." *Proceedings of the Dorset Natural History and Archaeological Society*, vol. 71 (1950), pp. 184–88.

———. "Mary Anning and the Fire at Lyme in 1844." *Proceedings of the Dorset Natural History and Archaeological Society*, vol. 74 (1953), pp. 175–77.

———. "Mary Anning and Anna Maria Pinney." *Proceedings of the Dorset Natural History and Archaeological Society*, vol. 76 (1955), pp. 146–52.

———. "Mary Anning's Escape from Lightning." *Proceedings of the Dorset Natural History and Archaeological Society*, vol. 80 (1959), pp. 91–93.

———. "Portraits of Mary Anning and Other Items." *Proceedings of the Dorset Natural History and Archaeological Society*, vol. 81 (1960), pp. 89–91.

———. "Mary Anning and a Very Small Boy." *Proceedings of the Dorset Natural History and Archaeological Society*, vol. 84 (1963), pp. 181–82.

Lendler, Ian. *The First Dinosaur: How Science Solved the Greatest Mystery on Earth*. New York, Margaret K. McElderry Books, 2019.

Maddox, Brenda. *Reading the Rocks: How Victorian Geologists Discovered the Secret of Life*. New York: Bloomsbury, 2017.

Mantell, Gideon Algernon. *The Medals of Creation, or First Lessons in Geology and in the Study of Organic Remains*. London: Henry Bohn, 1844.

———. "A Few Notes on the Prices of Fossils." *London Geological Journal and Record of Discoveries in British and Foreign Palaeontology*, vol. 1 (1846), pp. 13–17.

———. *Thoughts on a Pebble, or A First Lesson in Geology*. London: Reeve, Benham, and Reeve, 1849.

Miller, J. S. "Observations on Belemnites." *Transactions of the Geological Society*, series 2, vol. 2 (1829), pp. 45–62.

Owen, Richard. "A Description of Certain Belemnites, Preserved, with a Great Proportion of Their Soft Parts, in the Oxford Clay, at Christian-Malford, Wilts." *Philosophical Transactions of the Royal Society of London*, vol. 134 (1844), pp. 65–85.

Pascoe, Judith. *The Hummingbird Cabinet: A Rare and Curious History of Romantic Collectors*. Ithaca, NY: Cornell University Press, 2006.

Pierce, Patricia. *Jurassic Mary: Mary Anning and the Primeval Monsters*. Stroud, UK: History Press, 2016.

Pool, Daniel. *What Jane Austen Ate and Charles Dickens Knew: From Fox Hunting to Whist—The Facts of Daily Life in Nineteenth-Century England*. New York: Simon and Schuster, 1993.

Price, David. "Mary Anning Specimens in the Sedgwick Museum, Cambridge." *Geological Curator* 4, no. 6 (1986): pp. 319–24.

Riley, H. "On the Squaloraia." *Transactions of the Geological Society*, series 2, vol. 5 (1837): pp. 83–88.

Roberts, George. *The History of Lyme-Regis, Dorset, from the Earliest Periods to the Present Day.* London: Langdon and Barker, 1823.

———. *The History and Antiquities of the Borough of Lyme Regis and Charmouth.* London: Samuel Bagster and William Pickering, 1834.

Rudwick, Martin J. S. *Scenes from Deep Time: Early Pictorial Representations of the Prehistoric World.* Chicago: University of Chicago Press, 1995.

Taylor, Michael A. "Rediscovery of an Ichthyosaurus breviceps Owen, 1881 Sold by Mary Anning (1799–1847) to the Surgeon Astley Cooper (1768–1841) and Figured by William Buckland (1784–1856) in his Bridgewater Treatise." *Geoscience in South-West England*, vol. 13, pt. 3 (2014), pp. 321–27.

Taylor, Michael A., and Richard Bull. "A Token Found at Lyme Regis, Dorset, England, Apparently Associated with Mary Anning (1799–1847), Fossil Collector." *Proceedings of the Dorset Natural History & Archaeological Society*, vol. 136 (2015), pp. 63–67.

Taylor, Michael A., and Hugh S. Torrens. "An Account of Mary Anning (1799–1847), Fossil Collector of Lyme Regis, Dorset, England, Published by Henry Rowland Brown (1837–1921) in the Second Edition (1859) of Beauties of Lyme Regis." *Proceedings of the Dorset Natural History and Archaeological Society*, vol. 135 (2014), pp. 62–70.

———. "An Anonymous Account of Mary Anning (1799–1847), Fossil Collector of Lyme Regis, Dorset, England, Published in All The Year Round in 1865, and Its Attribution to Henry Stuart Fagan (1827/1890), Schoolmaster, Parson and Author." *Proceedings of the Dorset Natural History and Archaeological Society*, vol. 135 (2014), pp. 71–85.

———. "Saleswoman to a New Science: Mary Anning and the Fossil Fish Squaloraja from the Lias of Lyme Regis." *Proceedings of the Dorset Natural History and Archaeological Society*, vol. 108 (1987), pp. 135–48.

———. "An Anonymous Account of Mary Anning (1799–1847), Fossil Collector of Lyme
Regis, Dorset, England, Published in Chambers's Journal in 1857, and Its Attribution
to Frank Buckland (1826–1880), George Roberts (c. 1804–1860) and William Buckland (1784–1856)." *Archives of Natural History*, vol. 41 (2014), pp. 309–25.

Torrens, Hugh. "Mary Anning (1799–1847) of Lyme; 'The Greatest Fossilist the World Ever
Knew.'" *British Journal for the History of Science* 28, no. 3 (1995), pp. 257–84.

Institutions

Bristol University Library, Bristol, England: Archived materials of Anna Maria Pinney.

Cambridge University Library, Cambridge, England: Archived materials of Mary Anning.

Lyme Regis Museum, Lyme Regis, England: Exhibits associated with Mary Anning.

Natural History Museum, London, England: Exhibits and archived materials of Mary Anning.

Oxford University Museum of Natural History, Oxford, England: Exhibits and archived
materials of Mary Anning and Elizabeth Philpot.

Sedgwick Museum of Earth Sciences, Cambridge, England: Exhibits of Mary Anning materials.

IMAGE CREDITS

Title page

Plesiosaurus macrocephalus from Lyme Regis. Watercolor painting by George Scharf, 1838. Illustration from "A description of Viscount Cole's specimen of a *Plesiosaurus macrocephalus.*" *Transactions of the Geological Society of London,* series 2, vol. 5. Reproduced by permission of the Geological Society of London. (Also p. 67)

Contents

A Delineation of the Strata of England and Wales, with part of Scotland. Watercolor by William Smith, 1815. Reproduced by permission of the Geological Society of London. (Also p. 72)

Introduction

"*Temnodontosaurus* Fall." Mark Witton. (pp. viii–1)

Chapter 1. Crocodile or Sea Monster?

Ichthyosaurus (Temnodontosaurus) platyodon fossil. Natural History Museum, London. Copyright © Cheryl Blackford. (pp. 4–5)

Bullock's Museum. Illustration taken from *The Repository of Arts, Literature, Commerce, Manufactures, Fashions and Politics* by Rudolph Ackermann. British Library. (p. 6)

Chapter 2. Learning on the Beach

Lyme Regis. Engraving by J. Walker from an original drawing by J. Nixon, 1796. Courtesy of Lyme Regis Museum. (p. 9)

Anning family home. Drawing by W. H. Prideaux and Edward Liddon, 1842. Edward DuRose. (p. 10)

Black Ven. iStock.com/Cannasue. (p. 12)

Ammonite fossil. From the collection of Tom Sermon. (p. 14)

Ammonite. Peter Montgomery (paleopeter). (pp. 16–17)

Chapter 3. Not a Lady

Title page and text taken from a copy made by Mary Anning of a scientific paper about belemnites by J. S. Miller. Held in the Library and Archives, Natural History Museum, London. Copyright © Cheryl Blackford. (pp. 20, 88)

Henry De La Beche. Oil painting. National Museum of Wales. (p. 21)

William Buckland. Oil painting by Richard Ansdell, 1843. Reproduced by permission of the Geological Society of London. (p. 22)

Paris fashions, 1820. Anna Maria Pinney's scrapbook. Pinney archive held at the University of Bristol Special Collections DM58/Miscellaneous Volumes. Copyright © Cheryl Blackford. (p. 24)

Mary Anning. Pastel portrait by Benjamin John Merifield Donne, 1850. Reproduced by permission of the Geological Society of London. (p. 25)

Chapter 4. Geological Mysteries

Ichthyosaurus platyodon. Illustration in *Geology and Mineralogy Considered with Reference to Natural Theology,* vol. 2, by Rev. W. Buckland, 1836. Edward DuRose. (p. 28)

Proteosaurus, an ichthyosaur from Lyme Regis. Engraving by William Clift and James Basire, 1819. Reproduced by permission of the Geological Society of London. (p. 30)

Ichthyosaur preying on an ammonite. John Sibbick. (pp. 32–33)

Chapter 5. A Second Sea Monster

Cliffs near Lyme Regis. Nick Gardner. (p. 35)

Plesiosaurus dolichodeirus. Drawing by Mary Anning. Wellcome Library Collections. (pp. 38, 106)

Restoration of the *Plesiosaurus dolichodeirus* and *Ichthyosaurus communis.* Lithograph by George Scharf (from a drawing by William Conybeare). Illustration in "On the Discovery of an Almost Perfect Skeleton of the *Plesiosaurus*" by W. D. Conybeare, *Transactions of the Geological Society of London,* series 2, vol. 1 (1824). Reproduced by permission of the Geological Society of London. (p. 39)

Walter Thornbury and Edward Walford. iStock.com/whitemay. (p. 65)

Chapter 9. Radical Ideas

Duria Antiquior. Henry De La Beche, 1830. National Museum of Wales. (p. 74)

Copy of *On the Origin of Species by Means of Natural Selection* by Charles Darwin. Wellcome Library Collection. (p. 76)

Charles Darwin. University College London, Digital Collection. (p. 77)

Chapter 10. Legacy

Ichthyosaur fossil. Drawn by Mary Anning in a letter to Adam Sedgwick, 1843. Reproduced by kind permission of the Syndics of Cambridge University Library (DCU-6422). (p. 81)

Scholars attending a lecture in the Ashmolean Museum, Oxford. Lithograph by N. Whittock, Wellcome Library collection. (p. 85)

Temnodontosaurus platyodon fossil. Natural History Museum, London. Copyright © Cheryl Blackford. (pp. 86–87)

Glossary

Ammonite. From the collection of Tom Sermon. (p. 98)

Belemnites. Esther van Hulsen. (p. 98)

Ichthyosaurus. Esther van Hulsen. (p. 101)

Plesiosaurus. Esther van Hulsen. (p. 103).

Dimorphodon. Peter Montgomery (paleopeter). (p. 103)

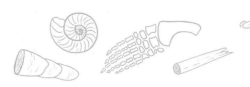

INDEX

Page numbers in **bold** indicate illustrations.